Easy Gourmet

MENUS TO LOWER YOUR

FAT THERMOSTAT™

Easy Gourmet

MENUS TO LOWER YOUR

FAT THERMOSTAT™

Written by
Chef Howard Gifford

Copyright 1991 by
Vitality House International, Inc.
1675 North Freedom Blvd, #11-C
Provo, Utah 84604

Telephone: 801-373-5100
To Order: Call Toll Free 1-800-637-0708

First Printing, April, 1991

This cookbook is a collection of recipes created by Chef Howard Gifford
to meet a no-sugar, low-fat, high complex carbohydrate criteria.

Library of Congress Catalog Card Number: 90-071128

ISBN 0-912547-08-1

Printed in the United States of America

Table of Contents

DEDICATION vi
ABOUT THE AUTHOR vii
ACKNOWLEDGEMENTS viii
FORWARD ix
SUGGESTED STAPLE PRODUCT x
EXPLANATION OF NUTRITIONAL INFORMATION xii

BEEF 1
Teriyaki Beef Tips with Whole Wheat Noodles 2
Mexican Chili Verde with Homemade Tortillas 8
Beef and Vegetable Turnover with Beef & Mushroom Sauce 17
"London Broil" with a Lite Beef Sauce 24
Gourmet Beef Strips in a Delicate Tomato Sauce 33
Yankee Style "Pot Roast" 39

CHICKEN 47
Old Fashioned Chicken and Dumplings 48
No Oil Crispy Fried Chicken 56
Honey Almond Chicken 64
Fried Chicken Steak with Country Gravy 72
Old Fashioned Chicken Pot Pie 79
Roast Chicken with a Plum Sauce 86
De-Lites Chicken Picante 94
De-Lites Gourmet Chicken 101

HOLIDAY 109
De-Licious Roast Chicken with Chicken Gravy 110
De-Licious Eggs Benedict 121
Spicy Turkey-Ham and Skillet Potatoes with Homemade Tortillas 127
Traditional Turkey Dinner with all the Trimmings 136
Baked Turkey-Ham with Pineapple Raisin Sauce 151

SEAFOOD 159
Paella (Seafood and Rice) 160
Fettuccine with Scallops Dijon 166
Louisiana Crab and Chicken Stew 173

SOUPS AND SALADS 179
Marinated Beef and Apple Salad 180
Fresh Green Salad 188
Chicken and Peach Salad 194
Cherry Sweet and Sour Beef Strip Salad 201

TURKEY 209
De-Licious Turkey Swiss Steak 210
De-Licious Ravioli with Tangy Tomato Sauce 218
Breast of Turkey Tiffany 227
Turkey Meatloaf Florentine with Monray Sauce 234

INDEX 241

DEDICATION

To my daughters, Britney and Starr. You both are my driving force. I love you both very much. This one's for you.

Dad

ABOUT THE AUTHOR

Chef Howard Gifford over the past several years has devoted his professional efforts to teaching, public service, and creating healthy, low-fat foods free of refined sugars or artificial sweeteners. Viewers of KSL Television's Eyewitness News at Noon over the past two years have responded enthusiastically to his low-fat cooking segment. As the driving force behind *Gifford's Gourmet De-Lites School of Cooking*, he offered a full teaching service on preparing healthy, low-fat foods for the average household. His first book, *Gifford's Gourmet De-Lites Complete Menu-Recipe Cookbook*, was well received when it was released nationwide in 1988.

Working closely with the Utah State Department of Health, Smith's Food and Drug Centers, KTVX television and various other sponsors, Chef Gifford plays a major roll in the "Change of Heart," program. This statewide campaign throughout the month of May offers cholesterol screenings, blood pressure screenings, cooking demonstrations, and general education designed to prevent heart disease in Utah. All of his time and labor throughout this campaign is donated. He is the creator of *Gifford's Gourmet De-Lites Spice Blends*, which were created to make cooking a little easier and the taste a little better.

Currently, Chef Gifford is involved in testing and recipe development for major food corporations, hospitals, restaurants, hotels, and other groups seeking healthier foods for their clients. He is featured in the soon to be released *Chef Gifford's "The Health Deck"* program and cooking video.

ACKNOWLEDGEMENTS

To my friend and close business associate, Dr. Edward Parent, who for many years has given his full support to many projects in our commitment to help those seeking a healthier lifestyle. The School of Cooking would not have been possible without him.

To Dr. Dennis Remington and Dr. Garth Fisher for their continued support.

To Steve Brown and Sydney Parent for all of the hard work they gave with layout and computerized production. A special thanks to Steve for the many cross-checks for errors.

To Barbara Higa who spent many hours computing the nutritional and food exchange information.

To Borge B. Andersen and Associates, Inc. for their masterful photography.

To Janet Schaap, food stylist, for her beautiful arrangements on the photos.

To Bill Kuhre, Kuhre Ad Art, for his art direction on the photos and all of the art work he did for the School of Cooking. What a masterful touch he has!

To my brother, Chef William Gifford, for all the hard work he has given at the School of Cooking. His assistance with testing and instruction with these menus made them successful. His gifted talents are awesome.

To Earl M. Johnson, President of Metropolitan Financial, Inc.. His gracious and enthusiastic support over the years has been greatly appreciated. I couldn't have asked for a better business advisor.

A special thanks, which is long overdue, goes out to Dr. Marcus Sorenson and his wife, Vicky, owners of The National Institute of Fitness. Many years ago they gave me the opportunity to be a part of their health resort where my career in the health field began.

And last, thanks to all of my students, past and present, and my television viewers. Their loyal support has been priceless.

FOREWORD

One of the more lighthearted comments I have received from the public over the years has been, "Chef, could you come home and prepare my meals?" My response, "Only if you do laundry." All in fun, Yes! But I had a thought. Wouldn't it be nice to spend a week in everyone's home? Sharing my techniques and ideas with them for a healthier lifestyle. Personally, I couldn't think of anything more gratifying, but this, of course, is impossible. My desire then is to be known as your "personal chef" through creating and developing recipes that fit in with your daily lifestyle.

All of the menus offered to you in this cookbook were developed and taught at my School of Cooking. My students at the school ranged from the single student, to the mother of four. And yes, even men would attend to learn how to organize and prepare healthy foods in their own kitchens. Many students would find comfort in seeing an instructional kitchen with average appliances, just like they had at home. All of the foods used are purchased at the supermarket. There are no secrets. So what all of my friends at the school receive, I can share with you in *Easy Gourmet Menus To Lower Your Fat Thermostat*. My spices have been created and then used in the recipes for taste and convenience. A spice substitute is also offered. Each menu has its own shopping list, which is broken down into seven categories:

1. Meats / Poultry / Seafood
2. Produce
3. Dairy
4. Frozen
5. Flours / Powders / Starches
6. Miscellaneous Groceries
7. Spices and Seasonings

This is very helpful while shopping. Remember to buy as many staple products as possible at one time. This will shorten each shopping list substantially. On the following pages I have included a suggested staple products list, with helpful hints on many of them. Remember that your commitment, dedication, and desire will harvest great rewards in your quest for a healthier lifestyle. Have fun in the kitchen, I sure do.

Your "Personal Chef"

Howard Gifford

SUGGESTED STAPLE PRODUCTS to buy in bulk and have on hand.

Meats / Poultry / Seafood

Beef Flank Steak - most flank steaks weigh 2 pounds. When buying purchase 4 to 6 pounds, or 3 steaks. At home, cut into 1 pound sections, re-wrap, identify, and freeze. If no flank steak is available, buy Tenderloin Steak as a substitute, but use caution because tenderloin has 4 additional grams of fat per 4 ounces.

Ground Turkey - cut into 1 pound sections if purchased in 10 pounds or more. Re-wrap, identify, and freeze unused sections.

Turkey-Ham - buy a 2 or 4 pound roll. Take roll to the butcher block. Ask store employee to slice ⅓ of roll into thin slices and to re-wrap both. Save the thin slices for breakfast menus and other uses.

Chicken - buy breasts in bulk. Re-wrap, identify, and freeze. When purchasing chicken tenders, follow above instructions.

Produce

The five most common fruits and vegetables used in food preparation.

Apples, Carrots, and Celery - hold up well. Also good to have always on hand, for emergency preparation and as a nutritional snack.

Onions - hold up well. One of the five fruits and vegetables that you should always have in your kitchen.

Potatoes - same as above. Also for a snack.

Dairy

Eggs - called for frequently. Should buy 2 dozen at a time.

Skim Milk and 1% Fat Cottage Cheese - determine your need. Buy only what you will use before the expiration date.

Ricotta Cheese - same as cottage cheese. Ricotta will hold up longer than cottage cheese.

Mozzarella Cheese - determine your need. Use before expiration date

Frozen

Juice Concentrates - buy a variety of what the cookbook calls for: Orchard Peach, Apple, Mountain Cherry, etc...Buy as many as you have room for in your freezer.
Frozen Berries and Vegetables - same as concentrates.

Flours / Powders / Starches

All should be on hand products.

Whole Wheat Flour
Oat Blend Flour
Oat Bran
Unprocessed Bran
Nonfat Milk Powder
Baking Powder
Baking Soda
Cornstarch

Miscellaneous Groceries

All Canned Goods - from tomato puree to crushed pineapple, canned goods in general have a long shelf life. Make a list and purchase as many as you can and have room for.
Lemon and Lime Juice
Worcestershire Sauce
Butter Bud Sprinkles - used frequently in recipes. Also good as a sprinkle for toast, potatoes, etc...
Grape Nuts - for breakfast, for a quick meal substitute, and for recipes. I always have a box on hand.
All Extracts
Raisins
Oil - there are many to choose from of vegetable origin. I prefer safflower oil when oil is called for.
Pickles - great for garnishes. Juice is called for in dressings etc... Long shelf life.
Unflavored Gelatin
Prepared Mustard
Vinegars - apple cider
Soy Sauce

Kitchen Bouquet - flavor enhancer and for color.
Rice - brown, long grain
Honey

Spices and Seasonings

Gifford's Spices - Dessert Spice, Basic Spice, Mexican Spice, Italian Spice, Chinese Spice, Gourmet Spice. These spices are used frequently in the recipes. To order Gifford's Spices see form in the back of this book.
Beef and Chicken Bouillon Granules- low sodium
Onion and Garlic Powder

*Buy remaining spices as called for with shopping lists.

Chef's note: By having all or some of these products available in your kitchen, shopping becomes very easy. You'll also find that shopping will become less frequent.

EXPLANATION OF NUTRITIONAL INFORMATION

Each recipe has nutritional information based on the scoring system featured in *How To Lower Your Fat Thermostat*. **RCU** stands for Refined Carbohydrate Units. 1 RCU = 6 grams of sugar or honey; 12 grams of white flour; 24 grams of raisins of dates, or 48 grams of concentrated fruit juice. According to Fat Thermostat guidelines you are allowed 2 RCU's per day. **FU** stands for Fat Unit. 1 FU= 6 grams of refined fat such as oil or margarine; or 8 grams of naturally occurring fat such as meat, milk, or eggs. You are allowed 4 FUs per day if your goal weight is less than 140 pounds and 5 FUs if it is more than 140 pounds.

Cal represents the number of calories in each serving, and %**Fat** represents the percentage of the total calories in that recipe derived from fat sources. **P, F,**and **C** represent the grams of protein, fat and carbohydrate respectively for each serving of the recipe. **Na** represents the number of milligrams of sodium in each serving. **T** indicates that there is only a trace (less than 1 gram) of a nutrient. For further information, refer to the Table of Food Composition, p. 187-208, in *How To Lower Your Fat Thermostat*.

Diabetic exchange information is also provided for each recipe. If you are a diabetic, consult your physician to see how you can fit the exchanges into your daily meal pattern.

Beef

MENU

Teriyaki Beef Tips with Whole Wheat Noodles
Crisp Chilled Chinese Vegetable Toss
Chef's Fruit Mold

Teriyaki Beef Tips with Whole Wheat Noodles

This has been a popular recipe in my supermarket demonstrations. For variety try seafood or chicken instead of beef.

½	C	lite soy sauce
3	T	Orchard Peach juice concentrate
3	T	apple juice concentrate, unsweetened
1	tsp	vegetable oil
2	tsp	Gifford's Chinese Spice
1	tsp	ground mustard
1	tsp	garlic powder
1	tsp	paprika
½	lb	beef flank steak, cut into ½ inch cubes
2	T	pimentos, diced
½	sm	yellow onion, diced
1	tsp	cornstarch, mixed with 1 T cold water, if necessary to thicken
12	oz	whole wheat noodles

Spice Substitute:

Instead of Gifford's Chinese Spice, substitute :

1	tsp	beef bouillon granules, low sodium
1	tsp	onion powder
1	tsp	ground ginger
½	tsp	allspice

1.   In a mixing bowl combine soy sauce, juice concentrates, oil, and spices. Whisk until smooth. Add beef cubes. Stir until well cooked.

Note: After preparing sauce; reserve ¼ C and set aside.

2.   Marinate for 15 minutes.

3.   Remove beef cubes from sauce. Place in skillet sprayed with a non-stick spray. Add onion. Saute over medium heat 10 minutes.

4.   Add the ¼ cup reserved sauce. Stir.

5.   Cook 5 additional minutes. Add pimentos. Stir. Add if necessary, the cornstarch mixture slowly stirring constantly to thicken. Serve over whole wheat noodles, cooked according to directions on package.

Yield: 4 servings

	RCU	FU	Cal	%Fat	P	F	C	Na
Per Serving	0	1	459	17	27	9	70	535

Per Serving = 1 Vegetable exchange; 4 Bread exchange; 1½ Meat exchange; 1 Fat exchange

Crisp Chilled Chinese Vegetable Toss

2	T	apple juice concentrate, unsweetened
1½	T	lite soy sauce
1	T	apple cider vinegar
1	tsp	honey
1	tsp	vegetable oil
½	tsp	Gifford's Chinese Spice
½	tsp	Gifford's Dessert Spice
8	oz	sliced water chestnuts, drained
6	oz	fresh or frozen pea pods
2	C	sliced chinese cabbage
1	C	torn red leaf lettuce
½	C	fresh bean sprouts
½	C	sliced fresh mushrooms
1	T	pimentos

Spice Substitute:

Instead of Gifford's Chinese and Dessert Spice, substitute :

½	tsp	onion powder
½	tsp	ground ginger
½	tsp	ground dry mustard
½	tsp	ground cinnamon
¼	tsp	allspice
1	tsp	dried lemon peel
1	tsp	dried orange peel
1	tsp	banana flavor extract

For dressing:

1. In a small mixing bowl combine apple juice concentrate, soy sauce, cider vinegar, honey, oil, and Gifford's Spices. Whisk until blended.

2. In a medium salad bowl combine water chestnuts, pea pods, cabbage, leaf lettuce, bean sprouts, mushrooms, and pimentos.

3. Pour dressing over salad, toss gently to coat vegetables. Chill a few minutes before serving.

    Yield: 4 servings

	RCU	FU	Cal	%Fat	P	F	C	Na
Per Serving	0	0	136	11	4	2	27	287

Per Serving = 3 Vegetable exchange

Chef's Fruit Mold

If you don't have a gelatin mold, a small baking dish or shallow bowl works nicely.

1	C	water
½	C	apple juice concentrate, unsweetened
1	T	lemon juice
1	T	dried lemon peel
1	T	unflavored gelatine
1	C	club soda
⅛	tsp	vanilla extract
1	sm	red apple, cored, cut in wedges
1	C	pineapple slices, drained, diced
1	sm	green apple, cored, peeled, chopped
½	C	halved seedless green grapes

1. Combine water, apple juice concentrate, lemon juice, and lemon peel in a small saucepan. Bring to a boil.

2. Dissolve unflavored gelatine in boiling mixture. Remove from heat. Cool to room temperature.

3. Slowly add club soda. Stir.

4. Arrange apple wedges and ½ of the pineapple in a 4½ cup mold. Pour in 1 cup of gelatine mixture. Chill until almost firm.

5. Chill remaining gelatine, in a separate bowl. When partially set, fold in remaining pineapple, chopped apple, and grapes. Pour over first layer. Chill until set.

6. Unmold onto plate. Cut into 4 servings. Serve over shredded lettuce if desired.

Yield: 4 servings

	RCU	FU	Cal	%Fat	P	F	C	Na
Per Serving	0	0	135	2	3	T	33	12

Per Serving = 2 Fruit exchange

Menu Shopping List

Teriyaki Beef Tips with Whole Wheat Noodles Menu

Meat
1	lb	beef flank steak

Produce
1	sm	yellow onion
1	sm	head Chinese cabbage
1	sm	head red leaf lettuce
6	oz	fresh pea pods, or 1-8oz pack frozen pea pods
2	oz	fresh bean sprouts
6	med	mushrooms
1	sm	red apple
1	sm	green apple
1	sm	bunch seedless green grapes

Frozen
1	12oz	can apple juice concentrate, unsweetened
1	12oz	can Orchard Peach juice concentrate

Flours / Powders / Starches
1	8oz	bag wide whole wheat noodles
1	sm	box cornstarch

Miscellaneous Groceries
1	8¼oz	can pineapple slices
1	12oz	club soda
1	8oz	can water chestnuts (sliced)
1	pint	apple cider vinegar
1	sm	bottle lite soy sauce
1	sm	bottle honey

1	sm	bottle vegetable oil
1	sm	bottle lemon juice
1	sm	bottle sliced pimentos
1	sm	box unflavored gelatin

Spices and Seasonings

1	bottle	garlic powder
1	bottle	dry ground mustard
1	bottle	paprika
1	bottle	lemon Peel
1	bottle	Gifford's Chinese Spice
1	bottle	Gifford's Dessert Spice

To order Gifford's Spices see form in the back of this book.

Instead of Gifford's Spices:

1	sm	jar beef bouillon granules, low sodium
1	bottle	onion powder
1	bottle	ground ginger
1	bottle	allspice
1	bottle	ground cinnamon
1	bottle	orange Peel
1	bottle	banana extract

Remember to check food products that you have on hand.

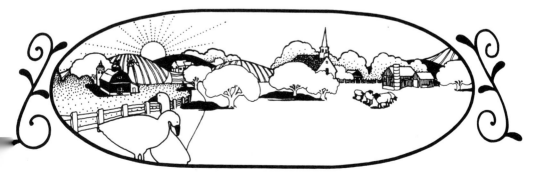

MENU

Mexican Chili Verde with Homemade Tortillas
Arroz Mexicano (Mexican Vegetable Rice)
Red Bean, Corn, and Melon Salad
Pina Colada Parfait with De-Lites Cream Cheese

Mexican Chili Verde

One of the favorite recipes of students at my School of Cooking, I feature a quicker version at supermarket demonstrations. How? In addition to the first seven ingredients add 1 cup Pace (mild) Picante Sauce and 1 Tablespoon of my Mexican Spice.

½	lb	beef flank steak, cut in 1-inch pieces
½	lb	chicken breasts, boneless, skinless, cut in 1-inch pieces
1	med	bell pepper, chopped
1	sm	onion, chopped
1	clove	garlic, minced
1	29oz	can whole tomatoes, cut-up and liquid reserved
1	4oz	can diced green chilies
⅓	C	fresh chopped parsley
½	C	water
¼	C	apple juice concentrate, unsweetened
1	T	lemon juice
1	T	lime juice
2	tsp	Gifford's Mexican Spice
1	tsp	beef bouillon granules, low sodium
1	tsp	chicken bouillon granules, low sodium
¼	tsp	Gifford's Dessert Spice

Spice Substitute:

Instead of Gifford's Mexican and Dessert Spice, substitute :

1	tsp	onion powder
1	tsp	garlic powder
1	tsp	chili powder
½	tsp	ground cumin
½	tsp	ground oregano
¼	tsp	ground cloves
dash		cinnamon

1. In a large skillet sprayed lightly with a non-stick spray combine beef and chicken. Cook over medium heat until brown.

2. Add bell pepper, onion, and garlic; stir. Simmer stirring occasionally until vegetables are tender.

3. In a large bowl combine tomatoes, chilies, parsley, water, apple juice concentrate, lemon juice, lime juice, and spices; stir to blend. Add mixture to skillet; stir. Simmer 15 minutes. Serve with tortillas.

Yield: 4 servings

	RCU	FU	Cal	%Fat	P	F	C	Na
Per Serving	0	1	258	29	29	5	24	393

Per Serving = ½ Fruit exchange; 2 Vegetable exchange; 3 Meat exchange

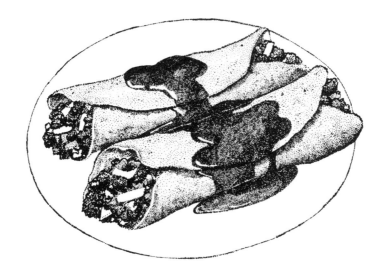

Homemade Tortillas

This recipe is as authentic as possible. It has no oils or shortenings. Since ancient times families in Old Mexico have enjoyed tortillas with most meals.

2	C	whole wheat flour
1	C	oat bran
2	tsp	baking powder
½	tsp	salt
		warm water (approximately 1 cup)

1. In a bowl stir together the flour, oat bran, baking powder and salt. Gradually stir in enough warm water to form a crumbly dough. Work the dough with your hands until it holds together.

2. Turn onto a board and knead the dough until smooth. Divide into 12 pieces and shape each into a smooth ball. Cover lightly with a plastic wrap and let rest for about 15 minutes.

3. For each tortilla, flatten ball into a 5 inch patty, then roll out into a 9-inch round tortilla, rolling from center to edge. Turn tortilla often, stretching the dough as you peel it from the board.

4. Place tortilla into a large, pre-heated, dry skillet over a medium-high heat. Tiny blisters will appear immediately.

5. Turn tortilla over and press directly on the top with a wide spatula. Press gently over all of tortilla. Turn and repeat. If tortillas stick or brown too quickly, reduce heat. Stack tortillas inside a folded towel and place inside a plastic bag until they become soft.

Yield: 12 9-inch tortillas

	RCU	FU	Cal	%Fat	P	F	C	Na
Per Tortilla	0	0	90	9	4	1	19	144

Per Tortilla = 1 Bread exchange

Arroz Mexicano (Mexican Vegetable Rice)

2½	C	water
½	sm	yellow onion, chopped fine
1	clove	garlic, minced
1	tsp	chicken bouillon granules, low sodium
1	tsp	Gifford's Mexican Spice
¼	tsp	Gifford's Dessert Spice
1	C	brown rice
1	10oz	box frozen peas and carrots

Spice Substitute:

Instead of Gifford's Mexican and Dessert Spice, substitute :

½	tsp	chili powder
½	tsp	cumin powder
½	tsp	onion powder
1	tsp	dried lemon peel
⅛	tsp	cinnamon
dash		red cayenne pepper

1. In a saucepan combine the water, chopped onion, minced garlic, and spices; bring to a boil. Stir in rice.

2. Bring back to full boil. Reduce heat to low and cover pan tightly; cook for 30 minutes. Do not remove cover throughout procedure.

3. Remove from heat, with cover still on tightly, let rice stand for 15 minutes.

4. In a separate saucepan cook peas and carrots according to package directions; drain. Add vegetables to rice. Gently fluff until blended. Serve.

Yield: 6 servings

	RCU	FU	Cal	%Fat	P	F	C	Na
Per Serving	0	0	148	5	5	1	34	68

Per Serving = 2 Bread exchange

Red Bean, Corn and Melon Salad

One of my personal favorites, I enjoy this with barbecues and other recipes as well.

4		red leaf lettuce leaves
2	C	shredded lettuce
1	15oz	can red beans, without sugar
1	C	frozen corn, thawed
1	16oz	bag frozen melon balls, thawed
1		lime , optional
½	tsp	Gifford's Mexican Spice
½	tsp	Gifford's Dessert Spice

Spice Substitute:

Instead of Gifford's Mexican and Dessert Spice, substitute :

½	tsp	chili powder
½	tsp	oregano
¼	tsp	cinnamon
⅛	tsp	ground nutmeg
1	tsp	dried orange peel

1.   Arrange red leaf onto 4 salad plates.

2.   Arrange ½ cup shredded lettuce onto each plate over red leaf.

3.   In a medium salad bowl combine red beans, corn, melon balls, and spices; stir to blend. Spoon mixture evenly onto salad plates over lettuce. Garnish with lime slices if desired. Serve.

Yield: 4 servings

	RCU	FU	Cal	%Fat	P	F	C	Na
Per Serving	0	0	221	6	12	1	44	47

Per Serving = ½ Fruit exchange; 2 Bread exchange

Pina Colada Parfait

For variety try this recipe with Orchard Peach juice concentrate, instead of pineapple juice concentrate. Also, add diced, or sliced, frozen peach slices, instead of crushed pineapple. Delicious!

½	C	water
1	env	unflavored gelatine
⅔	C	pineapple juice concentrate
⅓	C	water
1	tsp	imitation banana extract
1	tsp	coconut extract
1	tsp	almond extract
2	C	De-Lites Cream Cheese (see next recipe)
1	C	crushed pineapple, drained

1. Sprinkle unflavored gelatine over the ½ cup water; let stand 1 minute.

2. In a saucepan combine the Dole Pineapple juice concentrate, ⅓ cup water, and extracts; bring to a boil. Stir into gelatine mixture until completely dissolved. Chill until set.

3. When set, gently whip mixture. Using 4 parfait glasses, add 2 tablespoons cream cheese to bottom of each glass. Then add 2 tablespoons pineapple gelatine and 1 tablespoon crushed pineapple. Repeat procedure 3 times, or until glasses are full.

4. Top with a dollop of cream cheese. Sprinkle Gifford's Dessert Spice over top, if desired. Chill before serving.

Yield: 6 servings

	RCU	FU	Cal	%Fat	P	F	C	Na
Per Serving	0	0	166	5	11	1	26	174

Per Serving = ½ Milk exchange; 1½ Fruit exchange

De-Lites Cream Cheese

This recipe is often called for in the cookbook. Write it down on a card and place in the kitchen for easy access.

2	C	1% fat cottage cheese, reduced salt
¼	tsp	vanilla
1	T	honey
1	tsp	unflavored gelatin

1.   In a blender combine ingredients. Blend until smooth.

2.   Pour into a bowl with a tight fitting lid. Chill.

Yield: 1 pint

	RCU	FU	Cal	%Fat	P	F	C	Na
Per ¼ Cup	0	0	51	10	7	T	4	128

Menu Shopping List

Mexican Chili Verde Menu

Meat / Poultry
½	lb	beef flank steak
½	lb	boneless chicken breasts

Produce
1	med	bell pepper
2	sm	yellow onions
2	cloves	garlic
1	sm	bunch parsley
1	head	red leaf lettuce
1	sm	head iceberg lettuce

Dairy
1	pint	1% fat cottage cheese, reduced salt

Frozen
1	12oz	can apple juice concentrate, unsweetened
1	12oz	can pineapple juice concentrate
1	12oz	bag frozen unsweetened melon balls
1	sm	bag, of carton, frozen corn
1	sm	bag, or carton, peas and carrots

Miscellaneous Groceries
1	29oz	can Hunts Whole Tomatoes
1	4oz	can diced green chilies
1	sm	bottle lemon juice
1	sm	bottle lime juice
1	sm	bag whole wheat flour
1	box	oat bran cereal
1	sm	container baking powder
1	sm	bag long grain brown rice
1	15oz	can red beans, without sugar
1	sm	box unflavored gelatin

1	bottle	banana extract (imitation)
1	bottle	coconut extract
1	bottle	almond extract
1	sm	can crushed pineapple, unsweetened
1	bottle	vanilla
1	sm	container honey

Spices and Seasonings

1	sm	jar chicken bouillon granules, low sodium
1	sm	jar beef bouillon granules, low sodium
1	bottle	Gifford's Mexican Spice
1	bottle	Gifford's Dessert Spice

To order Gifford's Spices see form in the back of this book.

Instead of Gifford's Spices:

1	bottle	onion powder
1	bottle	garlic powder
1	bottle	chili powder
1	bottle	ground cumin
1	bottle	ground oregano
1	bottle	ground clove
1	bottle	ground cinnamon
		salt
1	bottle	lemon Peel
1	bottle	red cayenne pepper
1	bottle	ground nutmeg
1	bottle	orange Peel

Remember to check products you have on hand.

MENU

Beef and Vegetable Turnover with
Beef and Mushroom Sauce
Fruit Cocktail Salad
Fresh Tomato Slices on Red Leaf Lettuce
Fresh Strawberry Parfait

Beef and Vegetable Turnover Filling

The filling is a meal in itself. When in a hurry, microwave a potato. Cut lengthwise and press gently to form a pocket. Serve filling over top. Or, serve it in a whole-wheat pita pocket for a hearty lunch.

½	lb	beef flank steak, cut into small cubes
1	T	Butter Bud Sprinkles
2	T	whole wheat flour
⅔	C	water
½	sm	yellow onion, diced
1	stalk	celery , diced
1	12oz	package frozen peas and carrots, thawed---OR---
1	12oz	package frozen mixed vegetables, thawed
1	T	Gifford's Basic Spice
1½	tsp	beef bouillon granules, low sodium
3	T	tomato juice

Spice Substitute:

Instead of Gifford's Basic Spice, substitute :

1	tsp	onion powder
1	tsp	garlic powder
1	tsp	thyme
¼	tsp	black pepper
dash		ground nutmeg

1. In a skillet sprayed lightly with a non-stick spray saute beef cubes until browned.

2. With moisture still in the skillet from the beef cubes, sprinkle Butter Buds and whole wheat flour over beef; stir to blend. Add water. Stir to gather caramelizing from skillet. Reduce heat.

3. Add onions, celery, peas and carrots, spices, and tomato juice; stir. Simmer 10 minutes stirring occasionally.

Dough

⅔	C	whole wheat flour
⅓	C	oat bran
1	tsp	baking powder
¼	tsp	salt
2	lg	egg whites, slightly beaten
2	tsp	vegetable oil
¼	C	skim milk
2	T	Orchard Peach juice concentrate

1. In a mixing bowl combine wheat flour, oat bran, baking powder, and salt. Stir.

2. In a separate bowl combine egg whites, oil, skim milk, and Orchard Peach concentrate. Stir.

3. Add liquid mixture to flour mixture, stirring with a fork to blend.

4. Turn dough onto a well floured surface. Knead dough until smooth, adding small amounts of wheat flour while kneading if necessary. Cover and let rest a few minutes.

5. Separate dough into 4 parts. Roll each part into a ball. Roll out each ball in an oblong fashion until ¼ inch thick.

6. Spoon filling evenly to center of each turnover. Moisten edge and fold half of dough gently over filling until dough edges meet. Flute edges of turnover and fold in ½ inch.

7. Bake in a 450°F oven for 10 to 12 minutes, or until golden brown. Serve with Beef and Mushroom Sauce.

Yield: 4 turnovers.

	RCU	FU	Cal	%Fat	P	F	C	Na
Per Turnover	0	1	318	20	24	7	41	138

Per Turnover = 2 Bread exchange; 2 Meat exchange; 1 Fat exchange

Beef and Mushroom Sauce

2	C	water
1	T	Gifford's Basic Spice
1	tsp	beef bouillon granules, low sodium
1	C	fresh sliced mushrooms
1	T	cornstarch, mixed with small amount of cold water
2	T	low-fat evaporated milk
1	tsp	paprika, optional

Spice Substitute:

Instead of Gifford's Basic Spice, substitute :

2	tsp	beef bouillon granules, low sodium, additional
1	tsp	onion powder
½	tsp	garlic powder
½	tsp	ground mustard
dash		curry powder
dash		white pepper

1. In a saucepan combine the water, Basic Spice, beef bouillon granules and mushrooms; bring to a boil.

2. Reduce heat to simmer. Add cornstarch mixture slowly stirring constantly until thick. Add evaporated milk; stir. Simmer 5 minutes. Add 1 teaspoon paprika for color if desired. Spoon over beef turnovers or enjoy as a soup.
    Yield: approx. 2 cups

	RCU	FU	Cal	%Fat	P	F	C	Na
Per ¼ Cup	0	0	25	10	1	T	5	226

Fruit Cocktail Salad

Another favorite, it can be served with a variety of entrees. It's great for outings, barbecues, and picnics.

2	16oz	cans lite fruit cocktail, in pear juice, no sugar added, drained
1	C	De-Lites Cream Cheese (see recipe on page 14)
1		banana sliced
½	C	raisins
2	T	pineapple juice concentrate
1	tsp	Gifford's Dessert Spice
1	tsp	almond extract

Spice Substitute:

Instead of Gifford's Dessert Spice, substitute :

1	tsp	banana flavor extract
½	tsp	dried orange peel
½	tsp	ground cinnamon
⅛	tsp	ground all spice

1. Combine ingredients in a salad bowl. Gently fold ingredients until blended. Chill. Serve over lettuce if desired.

Yield: 6 servings

	RCU	FU	Cal	%Fat	P	F	C	Na
Per Serving	0	0	180	3	6	1	39	92

Per Serving = 2 Fruit exchange

Fresh Tomato Slices on Red Leaf Lettuce

3	med	tomatoes
8	leaves	red leaf lettuce
		Gifford's Basic Spice optional

1. Slice tomatoes. Arrange red leaf lettuce onto 4 salad plates, 2 each per plate. Place tomato slices over red leaf. Serve. Top off with Gifford's Basic Spice if desired.

Yield: 4 servings

	RCU	FU	Cal	%Fat	P	F	C	Na
Per Serving	0	0	23	11	1	T	5	10

Per Serving = 1 Vegetable Exchange

Fresh Strawberry Parfait

½	C	water
1	env	unflavored gelatine
⅔	C	Dole Country Raspberry juice concentrate
⅓	C	water
2	tsp	strawberry extract---OR---
2	tsp	cherry flavor extract
1	pint	fresh strawberries, sliced, reserve 4 whole strawberries for garnish
2	C	De-Lites Cream Cheese (see recipe on page 14)

1. In a bowl add the ½ cup water; sprinkle the unflavored gelatine over the top. Let stand 1 minute.

2. In a saucepan combine the Country Raspberry juice concentrate, ⅓ cup water, and extract; bring to a boil. Stir into gelatine mixture until completely dissolved; chill until set.

3. In a blender, puree ½ of the strawberries. Using 4 parfait glasses, add 2 tablespoons cream cheese to bottom of each glass. Then add 2 tablespoons strawberry puree. Repeat procedure 3 times finishing with strawberry puree at the top. Push down gently if needed to even ingredients in glasses. Top off with a dollop of cream cheese. Garnish with whole strawberry. Chill before serving.

Yield: 4 servings

	RCU	FU	Cal	%Fat	P	F	C	Na
Per Serving	0	0	234	7	17	2	36	274

Per Serving = 1 Milk exchange; 2 Fruit exchange

Menu Shopping List

Beef and Vegetable Turnover Menu

Meat
½	lb	beef flank steak

Produce
1	sm	yellow onion
1	sm	bunch celery
6	med	mushrooms
1		banana
3	med	tomatoes
1	sm	head Red leaf lettuce
1	pint	fresh strawberries

Dairy
1	qt	container 1% fat cottage cheese
1	pint	skim milk
1	doz	eggs (2 eggs required)

Frozen
1	12oz	can Orchard Peach juice concentrate
1	12oz	can Pineapple juice concentrate
1	12oz	can Country Raspberry juice concentrate
1	12oz	bag frozen peas and carrots --or--
1	12oz	bag mixed vegetables

Flours / Powders / Starches
1	sm	bag whole wheat flour
1	box	oat bran
1	sm	container baking powder
1	box	baking soda
1	box	cornstarch

Miscellaneous Groceries

1	bottle	Butter Bud Sprinkles
1	sm	can tomato juice
1	sm	bottle vegetable oil
1	can	low-fat evaporated milk
2	16oz	cans (lite) fruit cocktail, in pear juice
1	box	raisins
1	sm	box unflavored gelatin
1	sm	bottle honey
1	bottle	strawberry (or cherry) flavor extract
1	bottle	almond extract
1	bottle	vanilla

Spices and Seasonings

1	sm	jar beef bouillon granules, low sodium
		salt
1	bottle	Gifford's Basic Spice
1	bottle	Gifford's Dessert Spice

To order Gifford's Spices see form in the back of this book.

Instead of Gifford's Spices:

1	bottle	onion powder
1	bottle	garlic powder
1	bottle	thyme powder
1	bottle	black pepper
1	bottle	ground nutmeg
1	bottle	ground mustard
1	bottle	curry powder
1	bottle	white pepper
1	bottle	ground cinnamon
1	bottle	ground allspice
1	bottle	orange Peel
1	bottle	banana flavor extract

Remember to check products you have on hand.

MENU

"London Broil" with a Lite Beef Sauce
Seasoned Whole Baby Potatoes
Chilled Green Goddess Salad with
De-Lites Green Goddess Dressing
Buttery Oat Bran Muffins
Mountain Cherries Jubilee

"London Broil" with a Lite Beef Sauce

Here's an idea! Mix 1 cup De-Lites Cream Cheese gently together with 1 tsp onion powder and 1 tsp prepared horseradish for a "Creamy Horseradish Sauce." Serve over top. I love it!

1	lb	beef flank steak
½	C	beef broth, low sodium
1	T	vegetable oil
2	tsp	apple juice concentrate, unsweetened
2	tsp	red wine vinegar
2	tsp	Gifford's Basic Spice
½	tsp	Gifford's Dessert Spice
1	clove	garlic, minced

Spice Substitute:

Instead of Gifford's Basic and Dessert Spice, substitute:

2	tsp	onion powder
1	tsp	garlic powder
1	tsp	paprika
½	tsp	thyme
½	tsp	marjoram
⅛	tsp	ground cloves

1. Score steak on both sides.

2. Combine remaining ingredients in a bowl. Stir to blend.

3. Place flank steak in a shallow baking dish. Pour sauce over steak. Cover and marinade both sides for a few minutes.

Instructions for Broiling

4. Place on a unheated rack in a broiler pan. Broil 4 inches from heat for 5 minutes. Turn over and broil 5 more minutes. When serving carve steak diagonally, across grain, into very thin slices.

Instructions for Grilling

4. Pre-heat a griddle or a skillet over medium-high heat. Cook steak on one side for 4 minutes. Turn and cook another 4 minutes. When serving carve steak diagonally, across grain, into very thin slices.

Sauce

2	C	water
1	T	Gifford's Basic Spice
1½	tsp	beef bouillon granules, low sodium
1	T	cornstarch, mixed with 3 T cold water

Spice Substitute:

Instead of Gifford's Basic Spice, substitute:

1	tsp	onion powder
1	tsp	thyme
½	tsp	garlic powder
1	tsp	Butter Bud Sprinkles
pinch		white pepper

5. In a saucepan bring the water, Basic Spice, and beef granules to a boil. Reduce heat to simmer.

6. Slowly add cornstarch mixture and stir constantly until mixture thickens.

7. Pour over beef slices when serving, or serve in a cup and dip beef in sauce.

Yield: 4 servings; approx. ½ cup each

	RCU	FU	Cal	%Fat	P	F	C	Na
Per Serving	0	1	235	20	25	10	9	193

Per Serving = 3 Meat exchange; 2 Fat exchange

Seasoned Whole Baby Potatoes

2	15oz	cans whole new potatoes, drained
		Butter Bud Sprinkles to taste
		Gifford's Basic Spice to taste

Spice Substitute:

Instead of Gifford's Basic Spice, substitute:

1	tsp	onion powder
1	tsp	garlic powder
1	tsp	chicken bouillon granules, low sodium
½	tsp	paprika
½	tsp	thyme
½	tsp	black pepper

Mix together in small bowl, and use as directed.

1. Arrange potatoes in a baking dish that has been sprayed lightly with a non-stick spray. Sprinkle Butter Buds and Basic Spice evenly over potatoes.

2. Bake in a 375°F oven for 25 to 30 minutes. Serve.

Yield: 4 to 6 servings

	RCU	FU	Cal	%Fat	P	F	C	Na
Per Serving	0	0	95	2	3	T	22	8

Per Serving = 1 Bread exchange

Chilled Green Goddess Salad

1	sm	head romaine lettuce, torn into small pieces
1	sm	head red leaf lettuce, torn into small pieces
1	4oz	can artichoke hearts, drained, reserve liquid
2	med	tomatoes, cut into wedges
½	sm	red onion, cut julienne
½	tsp	Gifford's Basic Spice
½	tsp	Gifford's Italian Spice

Spice Substitute:

Instead of Gifford's Basic and Italian Spice, substitute:

1	tsp	garlic powder
1	tsp	onion powder
½	tsp	thyme
½	tsp	basil
½Ttsp		ground fennel
¼	tsp	black pepper

Mix spices together, then use as directed.

1. In a large salad bowl combine all ingredients. Toss gently to blend.

2. Cover and chill a few minutes. Serve.

Yield: 4 servings

	RCU	FU	Cal	%Fat	P	F	C	Na
Per Serving	0	0	72	10	5	1	15	58

Per Serving = 2 Vegetable exchange

De-Lites Green Goddess Dressing

1½	C	1% cottage cheese, reduced salt
1	T	honey
⅛	tsp	vanilla
½	C	loosely packed parsley leaves
1		green onion, cut up
2	T	reserved artichoke heart juice
2	T	Peach juice concentrate
1	T	tarragon vinegar
1	T	onion powder
½	tsp	Gifford's Gourmet Spice
½	tsp	Gifford's Italian Spice

Spice Substitute:

Instead of Gifford's Gourmet and Italian Spice, substitute:

½	tsp	crushed tarragon leaves
½	tsp	dill weed
½	tsp	basil
½	tsp	thyme
½	tsp	garlic powder
2	tsp	chicken bouillon granules, low sodium
dash		ground cloves

1. In a blender combine all ingredients. Blend until smooth. Chill before serving.

    Yield: approx. 1 pint

	RCU	FU	Cal	%Fat	P	F	C	Na
Per ¼ Cup	0	0	59	9	6	1	7	245

Buttery Oat Bran Muffins

Altitudes vary across the country. If muffins do not rise enough, increase baking powder and baking soda by half.

1¾	C	oat bran
1	C	unprocessed bran
3	T	Butter Bud Sprinkles
1½	tsp	baking powder
½	tsp	baking soda
1	tsp	Gifford's Dessert Spice
¼	tsp	salt
2	lg	egg whites
⅓	C	Mountain-Cherry juice concentrate
1½	tsp	vegetable oil
1½	C	skim milk

Spice Substitute:

Instead of Gifford's Dessert Spice, substitute:

¼	tsp	ground cinnamon
⅛	tsp	allspice
1	tsp	banana flavor extract

1. In a large mixing bowl combine the oat bran, unprocessed bran, Butter Bud Sprinkles, baking powder, baking soda, Dessert Spice, and salt. Blend well.

2. Make a well in center of flour mixture. Add remaining ingredients to the well. Stir gently until blended.

3. Spray a teflon muffin pan lightly with a non-stick spray. Spoon mixture into muffin pan, filling each cup ⅔ cup full.

4. Bake in oven at 375°F for 20 to 25 minutes, or until golden brown. *Yield:* 12 muffins

	RCU	FU	Cal	%Fat	P	F	C	Na
Per Muffin	0	0	84	20	5	2	15	194

Per Muffin = 1 Bread exchange

Mountain Cherries Jubilee

This is fantastic as a topping on cheesecake, puddings, cobblers, sorbet, muffins, etc. All of which are in this cookbook. It is also great when served over pancakes. See my first cookbook, Gifford's Gourmet De-Lites.

1	16oz	can pitted red tart pie cherries, packed in water
⅔	C	Mountain Cherry juice concentrate
2	tsp	cherry flavor extract
½	tsp	almond flavor extract
1	tsp	Gifford's Dessert Spice
1	T	cornstarch, mixed with 3 T cold water
		oat bran graham crackers, to garnish

Spice Substitute:

Instead of Gifford's Dessert Spice, substitute:

½	tsp	black walnut extract
¼	tsp	ground cinnamon
⅛	tsp	ground anise seed

1. In a saucepan bring to a boil the cherries, Mountain Cherry juice concentrate, cherry extract, almond extract, and Dessert Spice.

2. Slowly add cornstarch mixture and stir constantly until mixture thickens. Remove from heat.

3. Spoon mixture into 4 dessert dishes. Garnish with 4 oat bran graham crackers for each serving. Best if served warm.

    Yield: 4 servings

	RCU	FU	Cal	%Fat	P	F	C	Na
Per Serving	0	0	139	2	1	T	33	20

Per Serving = 2 Fruit exchange

Menu Shopping List

"London Broil" with a Lite Beef Sauce Menu

Meat
1   lb   beef flank steak

Produce
1   sm   head romaine lettuce
1   sm   head red leaf lettuce
2   med   tomatoes
1   sm   red onion
1   sm   bunch parsley
1   sm   bunch green onions
1   bud   garlic

Dairy
1   pint   1% fat cottage cheese
1   doz   eggs (2 eggs required)
1   pint   skim milk

Frozen
1   12oz   can apple juice concentrate, unsweetened
1   12oz   can Orchard Peach juice concentrate
1   12oz   can Mountain Cherry juice concentrate

Flours / Powders / Starches
1   box   cornstarch
1   box   oat bran cereal
1   box   unprocessed bran
1   sm   container baking powder
1   box   baking soda

Miscellaneous Groceries
1   sm   bottle red wine vinegar
1   bottle   tarragon vinegar (if not found with other vinegars, check specialty foods section)

1	sm	bottle vegetable oil
1	bottle	Butter Bud Sprinkles
2	15oz	cans whole new potatoes (Hunts preferred)
1	4oz	can artichoke hearts
1	sm	container honey
1	sm	bottle vanilla
1	16oz	can red tart pie cherries, packed in water
1	box	oat bran graham crackers (check in specialty foods section)
1	bottle	banana extract
1	bottle	cherry flavor extract
1	bottle	almond flavor extract
1	bottle	black walnut extract

Spices and Seasonings

1	sm	jar beef bouillon granules, low sodium
1	sm	jar chicken bouillon granules, low sodium
1	bottle	Gifford's Basic Spice
1	bottle	Gifford's Dessert Spice
1	bottle	Gifford's Italian Spice
1	bottle	Gifford's Gourmet Spice

Instead of Gifford's Spices:

1	bottle	onion powder
1	bottle	garlic powder
1	bottle	paprika
1	bottle	ground thyme
1	bottle	marjoram
1	bottle	ground cloves
1	bottle	white pepper
1	bottle	black pepper
1	bottle	basil
1	bottle	ground fennel (if not available, grind fennel in blender)
1	bottle	crushed tarragon
1	bottle	dill weed
1	bottle	ground cinnamon
1	bottle	ground anise seed

MENU

Gourmet Beef Strips in a Delicate Tomato Sauce
De-Lites Mashed Potatoes
Steamed Broccoli with Creamy Hollandaise Sauce
Chilled Boysenberries with De-Lites Cream Cheese

Beef Strips in a Delicate Tomato Sauce

½	lb	beef flank steak, cut into thin strips
½	sm	yellow onion, cut julienne
4	med	mushrooms, sliced
1	C	tomato juice
1	T	Orchard Peach juice concentrate
1	T	Gifford's Gourmet Spice
1	tsp	beef bouillon granules, low sodium

Spice Substitute:

Instead of Gifford's Gourmet Spice, substitute:

1	tsp	beef bouillon granules, low sodium, additional
2	tsp	onion powder
1	tsp	garlic powder
½	tsp	dill weed
½	tsp	crushed tarragon leaves
¼	tsp	ground fennel seed
⅛	tsp	ground cloves

1. Brown beef strips in a saucepan over medium-high heat.

2.   Add onions. Stir. Reduce heat. Saute beef strips and onions until onions are tender.

3.   Add mushrooms, tomato juice, and peach concentrate. Stir to blend. Add Gourmet Spice and beef bouillon granules. Stir.

4.   Reduce heat to low. Cook for 10 minutes stirring occasionally. Serve.

Yield: 4 servings

	RCU	FU	Cal	%Fat	P	F	C	Na
Per Serving	0	½	122	26	13	4	9	150

Per Serving = ½ Vegetable exchange; 1½ Meat exchange; ½ Fat exchange

De-Lites Mashed Potatoes

One of my students claimed that these mashed potatoes were the best she had ever eaten. They are good.

2	lg	potatoes, peeled and cut into small pieces
2	C	water
1½	T	Butter Bud Sprinkles
2	tsp	onion powder
1	tsp	chicken bouillon granules, low sodium
dash		white pepper
½	C	low-fat evaporated milk

1.   Place the potatoes and water in a saucepan and bring to a boil. Reduce heat. Cover.

2.   Simmer 12 minutes, or until potatoes are tender. Drain. Remove cover.

3.   Add remaining ingredients. Reduce heat to low.

4.   Mash potato mixture right in the pan, using a wire whip, or a potato masher. Remove from heat. Serve. An electric hand mixer can also be used.

Yield: 4 servings

	RCU	FU	Cal	%Fat	P	F	C	Na
Per Serving	0	0	98	2	5	T	20	44

Per Serving = 1 Bread exchange

Steamed Broccoli with Creamy Hollandaise Sauce

1	med	bundle fresh broccoli---OR---
1	16oz	bag frozen cut broccoli

1. Steam broccoli in ¼ cup of water until broccoli is tender.

Sauce

1	C	De-Lites Cream Cheese (see recipe on page 14)
1	tsp	lemon juice
1	tsp	onion powder
½	tsp	chicken bouillon granules, low sodium
1	tsp	prepared mustard

1. In a small mixing bowl combine ingredients. Stir gently to blend.

2. Let sauce stand at room temperature a few minutes. Spoon over broccoli when serving. Can be heated in microwave if desired on low setting.

Yield: 1¼ cup, 5 servings

	RCU	FU	Cal	%Fat	P	F	C	Na
Per Serving	0	0	124	11	15	1	14	212

Per Serving = 1 Vegetable exchange

Chilled Boysenberries and De-Lites Cream Cheese

1	16oz	bag frozen boysenberries, thawed
1	C	De-Lites Cream Cheese (see recipe on page 14)

1.   Place boysenberries into 4 dessert dishes, with juice. Spoon cream cheese over top. Serve.

Note: Sprinkle Gifford's Dessert Spice over top if desired.

Yield: 4 servings

	RCU	FU	Cal	%Fat	P	F	C	Na
Per Serving	0	0	120	7	8	1	20	131

Per Serving = 1 Fruit exchange

Menu Shopping List

Gourmet Beef Strips in a
Delicate Tomato Sauce Menu

Meat
½ lb beef flank steak

Produce
1 sm yellow onion
4 med onions
2 lg potatoes
1 bunch broccoli

Dairy
1 pint 1% fat cottage cheese, reduced salt

Frozen
1 sm can Orchard Peach juice concentrate
1 bag frozen broccoli (if not using fresh)
1 16oz bag frozen boysenberries

Miscellaneous Groceries
1 sm can tomato juice
1 bottle Butter Bud Sprinkles
1 sm can low-fat evaporated milk
1 sm jar prepared mustard
1 sm bottle lemon juice
1 sm container honey
1 bottle vanilla
1 sm box unflavored gelatin

Spices and Seasonings
1 sm jar beef bouillon granules, low sodium
1 sm jar chicken bouillon granules, low sodium

| 1 | bottle | Gifford's Gourmet Spice |
| 1 | bottle | Gifford's Dessert Spice |

To order Gifford's Spices see form in the back of this book.

Instead of Gifford's Spices:

1	bottle	onion powder
1	bottle	garlic powder
1	bottle	dill weed
1	bottle	crushed tarragon
1	bottle	ground fennel
1	bottle	ground cloves
1	bottle	white pepper

Remember to check products on hand.

MENU

Yankee Style "Pot Roast"
Fresh Garden Salad with
De-Lites Thousand Isle Dressing
Steamed Cut Green Beans
De-Lites Peach Cobbler

Yankee Style "Pot Roast"

We got a very positive response from viewers when I featured this recipe on television. I trust it will become one of your favorites. Yes, we can have our beef and a healthy lifestyle too!

½	C	whole wheat flour
1	T	Gifford's Basic Spice
1	tsp	beef bouillon granules, low sodium
1	lb	beef flank steak, tenderized
1	C	beef broth, low sodium
½	C	tomato juice
1	tsp	dried basil
1	T	worcestershire sauce
1	16oz	bag frozen stew vegetables

Spice Substitute:

Instead of Gifford's Basic Spice, substitute:

1	tsp	beef bouillon granules, low sodium, additional
2	tsp	onion powder
1	tsp	garlic powder
1	tsp	thyme
1	tsp	paprika
¼	tsp	black pepper

1.   Combine flour, Basic Spice, and bouillon granules in a blender. Blend until smooth. Place mixture in a shallow dish.

2.   Roll-up beef flank tightly. Thoroughly cover beef steak in flour mixture, including edges of beef roll.

3.   On medium high heat brown the beef roll evenly in a skillet sprayed lightly with a non-stick spray. Drop a tablespoon of beef broth around and between beef roll frequently, to help browning procedure.

4.   When beef roll is browned, add remaining broth, tomato juice, basil, and worcestershire sauce. Stir gently to blend around beef roll.

5.   Add the stew vegetables. Stir to blend evenly.

6.   Reduce heat slightly and cover. Simmer for 30 minutes stirring occasionally. Add additional beef broth if needed. Remove from heat.

7.   Remove beef roll from skillet. Slice beef roll into ¼ inch slices. Place slices onto serving plates.

8.   Spoon vegetables around beef slices. Spoon sauce over all. Serve.

Yield: 4 servings; approx. 3 beef slices, or 3 oz. each

	RCU	FU	Cal	%Fat	P	F	C	Na
Per Serving	0	2	378	37	29	16	31	460

Per Serving = 1 Vegetable exchange; 1½ Bread exchange; 3 Meat exchange; 1 Fat exchange

Fresh Garden Salad

See recipe on page 188.

De-Lites Thousand Isle Dressing

1	C	1% fat cottage cheese, reduced salt
1	med	dill pickle, kosher, crunchy, half the salt

2	T	dill pickle juice
1	med	celery stalk, cut-up
4	T	tomato puree
1	T	Gifford's Basic Spice
2	T	apple juice concentrate, unsweetened

Spice Substitute:

Instead of Gifford's Basic Spice, substitute:

2	tsp	beef bouillon granules, low sodium
2	tsp	onion powder
1	tsp	garlic powder
1	tsp	thyme
1	tsp	paprika
¼	tsp	white pepper

1. Combine all ingredients in a blender. Blend until smooth, about 1 minute. Chill if desired. Serve.

Yield: 1½ cups

	RCU	FU	Cal	%Fat	P	F	C	Na
Per ¼ Cup	0	0	55	10	6	T	7	209

Steamed Cut Green Beans

1   16oz   bag frozen cut green beans

1. Steam beans according to directions on package.

Yield: 4 servings

	RCU	FU	Cal	%Fat	P	F	C	Na
Per Serving	0	0	37	6	2	T	9	3

Per Serving = 1 Vegetable exchange

De-Lites Peach Cobbler

A rich, satisfying dessert. You will feel like you're cheating. There's only 9% fat per serving though. It doesn't get any better than this.

1	16oz	bag frozen peach slices, no sugar added
⅓	C	Orchard Peach juice concentrate
2	T	apple juice concentrate, unsweetened
1	tsp	Gifford's Dessert Spice
2	tsp	cornstarch, mixed with 2 T cold water

Spice Substitute:

Instead of Gifford's Dessert Spice, substitute:

1	tsp	ground cinnamon
¼	tsp	ground clove

1. In a saucepan combine the peaches, Orchard Peach juice concentrate, apple juice concentrate, and Dessert Spice. Bring to a boil.

2. Slowly add cornstarch mixture stirring constantly until mixture thickens. Reduce heat at once.

3. Pour mixture into a shallow baking dish. Set aside and keep warm.

Dough

⅔	C	whole wheat flour
⅓	C	oat bran
2	tsp	baking powder
dash		salt
2	lg	egg whites, slightly beaten
2	T	skim milk
3	T	Orchard Peach juice concentrate
1	tsp	vegetable oil
		De-Lites cream cheese, optional (see recipe on page 14)

4. In a bowl combine wheat flour, oat bran, baking powder, and salt. Stir.

5.   In separate bowl combine egg whites, skim milk, juice concentrate, and oil. Stir. Add to flour mixture stirring with fork until combined.

6.   Drop dough a tablespoon at a time directly onto peach mixture in baking dish. Cover. Bake in a 350°F oven for 30 minutes.

7.   Spoon mixture evenly into serving dishes. Top with De-Lites cream cheese if desired.

Yield: 4 servings

	RCU	FU	Cal	%Fat	P	F	C	Na
Per Serving	0	0	242	9	7	2	52	246

Per Serving = 2 Fruit exchange; 1 Bread exchange

Menu Shopping List

Yankee Style "Pot Roast" Menu

Meat
1	lb	beef flank steak

Produce
1	sm	head iceberg lettuce
1	sm	head red leaf lettuce
1	pint	cherry tomatoes
1	sm	bunch celery

Dairy
1	doz	eggs (2 eggs required)
1	pint	skim milk
1	pint	1% fat cottage cheese, reduced salt

Frozen
1	16oz	bag frozen stew vegetables
1	12oz	can frozen apple juice concentrate
1	16oz	bag frozen cut green beans
1	sm	can Orchard Peach juice concentrate
1	16oz	bag frozen peach slices, unsweetened

Flours / Powders / Starches
1	sm	bag whole wheat flour
1	box	oat bran cereal
1	box	cornstarch
1	sm	container baking powder

Miscellaneous Groceries
1	sm	can tomato juice
1	bottle	worcestershire sauce
1	sm	jar dill pickles
1	sm	can tomato puree
1	bottle	vegetable oil

Spices and Seasonings

1	sm	jar beef bouillon granules, low sodium
1	bottle	Gifford's Basic Spice
1	bottle	Gifford's Dessert Spice

To order Gifford's Spices see form in the back of this book.

Instead of Gifford's Spices:

1	bottle	onion powder
1	bottle	garlic powder
1	bottle	thyme
1	bottle	paprika
		black pepper
1	bottle	white pepper
1	bottle	ground cinnamon
1	bottle	ground cloves

Remember to check your products on hand.

Chicken

MENU

Old Fashioned Chicken and Dumplings
Chilled Endive Salad and
A Lite Cherry-Lemon Dressing
De-Lites Hot Bran Muffins
Steamed Cut Green Beans
Mandarin Orange Gelatin Dessert

Old Fashioned Chicken and Dumplings

My students at the Cooking School couldn't believe this was low-fat. Part of my objective when presenting recipes such as this is to tear down the wall of belief that you can't eat traditional meals while losing and maintaining weight. I can't state enough how much fun I have demonstrating these recipes.

4		chicken breasts, skinless, cut in half
4		chicken thighs, skinless
4		chicken legs, skin removed and discarded
3	stalks	celery, cut into 1 inch pieces
3	lg	carrots, peeled, cut into 1 inch pieces
2	med	potatoes, quartered, then cut into 1 inch pieces
1	lg	onion, cut into 1 inch pieces
2	T	Gifford's Basic Spice
1	T	chicken bouillon granules , low sodium
		Enough water to cover ingredients; then add 2 C more water

Spice Substitute:

Instead of Gifford's Basic Spice, substitute:

2	T	onion powder
½	tsp	garlic powder

½	tsp	ground thyme
¼	tsp	white pepper

1. In a large stock pot combine all ingredients. Stir. Bring to a boil. Cover pan and reduce heat to a simmer. Cook for 25 minutes.

Dumplings

1	C	whole wheat flour
2	tsp	baking powder
dash		salt
1	T	fresh chopped parsley
2	lg	egg whites, slightly beaten
¼	C	skim milk
1	tsp	vegetable oil

Chef's note: Prepare dumplings when cooking time for the chicken is almost expired.

2. Stir together the flour, baking powder, salt, and parsley.

3. In a separate bowl combine the egg whites, milk, and oil. Add to flour mixture stirring with a fork until just combined.

4. Remove cover from chicken. Drop dumpling dough from a tablespoon directly onto broth. Return cover to pan. Simmer an additional 10 minutes, do not remove cover. Remove chicken, vegetables, and dumplings from pan, to a serving dish; keep warm. Strain broth into a saucepan.

Gravy

		broth from chicken
2	T	cornstarch, mixed with ⅓ C cold water
1	C	low-fat evaporated milk

5. Bring broth to a boil. Add cornstarch mixture slowly stirring constantly until sauce thickens. Reduce heat. Add milk. Stir and simmer 5 minutes.

6.   Spoon gravy over chicken, vegetables, and dumplings when serving.

   Yield: 4 servings

	RCU	FU	Cal	%Fat	P	F	C	Na
Per Serving	0	1	433	12	37	6	60	365

Per Serving = ½ Milk exchange; 1 Vegetable exchange; 2 Bread exchange; 2½ Meat exchange

Chilled Endive Salad

1	lg	head endive lettuce, torn into small pieces
10		cherry tomatoes, cut in half
½	sm	red onion, cut julienne
½	tsp	Gifford's Basic Spice
¼	tsp	Gifford's Gourmet Spice

Spice Substitute:

Instead of Gifford's Basic and Gourmet Spice, substitute:

In a small dish mix together:

¼	tsp	onion powder
¼	tsp	garlic powder
¼	tsp	ground thyme
¼	tsp	dill weed
⅛	tsp	black pepper

1.   Combine torn lettuce, tomatoes, and onion in a salad bowl.

2.   Mix spices together, sprinkle over salad. Toss salad gently until mixed. Serve.

   Yield: 4 servings

	RCU	FU	Cal	%Fat	P	F	C	Na
Per Serving	0	0	27	11	2	T	6	10

Per Serving = 1 Vegetable exchange

A Lite Cherry-Lemon Dressing

At the end of a class I was asked to show how I come up with recipe ideas. The products in this recipe were already out on the counter. Voila! Here it is.

1	C	1% fat cottage cheese, reduced salt
⅓	C	Mountain Cherry juice concentrate
1	tsp	lemon juice
1	T	Butter Bud Sprinkles
1	tsp	Gifford's Dessert Spice
1	tsp	dried lemon peel

Spice Substitute:

Instead of Gifford's Dessert Spice, substitute:

½	tsp	ground cinnamon
¼	tsp	ground clove
⅛	tsp	nutmeg
1	tsp	dried orange peel

1. Combine all ingredients in a blender. Mix until smooth. Chill. Spoon over endive salad.

   Yield: approx. 1½ cups

	RCU	FU	Cal	%Fat	P	F	C	Na
Per ¼ Cup	0	0	55	8	5	.5	8	157

Per ¼ Cup = ½ Fruit exchange

De-Lites Hot Bran Muffins

2	C	unprocessed bran
1	C	whole wheat flour
1½	tsp	baking powder
½	tsp	baking soda
¼	tsp	salt

2	lg	egg whites, slightly beaten
1½	C	skim milk
¼	C	apple juice concentrate, unsweetened
2	T	honey
2	tsp	vegetable oil

1. Stir together the bran, wheat flour, baking powder, baking soda, and salt. Make a well in center of dry ingredients.

2. Add remaining ingredients to the well. Stir gently until blended.

3. Spray a teflon muffin pan lightly with a non-stick spray. Spoon mixture into muffin pan, filling each cup almost to the top. Bake at 375°F for 20 minutes, or until muffins are golden brown.

   Yield: 12 Muffins

	RCU	FU	Cal	%Fat	P	F	C	Na
Per Muffin	0	0	87	15	5	2	18	193

Per Muffin = 1 Bread exchange

Steamed Cut Green Beans

| 1 | 16oz | bag frozen cut green beans |
| 2 | T | diced pimentos |

1. Steam beans and pimentos in small amount of water, covered, 7 minutes. Drain. Serve.

   Yield: 4 servings

	RCU	FU	Cal	%Fat	P	F	C	Na
Per Serving	0	0	40	6	2	T	9	6

Per Serving = 1 Vegetable exchange

Pictured: Teriyaki Beef Tips with Whole Wheat Noodles, Crisp Chilled Chinese Vegetable Toss, and Chef's Fruit Mold, p. 2

Mandarin Orange Gelatin Dessert

If you can't find mandarin orange sections in juice concentrate, use a small orange.

½	C	cold water
1	env	unflavored gelatin
1	C	Mandarin Tangerine juice concentrate
11	oz	mandarin orange sections, in juice concentrate, unsweetened, drained
1	T	dried orange peel
1	tsp	Gifford's Dessert Spice
		De-Lites cream cheese, optional (see recipe on page 14)

Spice Substitute:

Instead of Gifford's Dessert Spice, substitute:

½	tsp	black walnut extract
¼	tsp	ground cinnamon
		pinch of allspice

1. In a medium bowl sprinkle unflavored gelatin over cold water. Let stand 1 minute.

2. In a saucepan bring to a boil the 1 cup mandarin tangerine juice concentrate. Add to gelatin and stir until completely dissolved. Stir in orange peel and Dessert Spice.

3. Pour mixture into 4 dessert dishes. Chill until consistency of unbeaten egg whites. Fold in mandarin orange sections evenly into dishes. Chill until firm. Top off with a teaspoon of De-Lites Cream Cheese when serving, if desired.

    Yield: 4 servings

	RCU	FU	Cal	%Fat	P	F	C	Na
Per Serving	0	0	147	1	4	T	34	7

Per Serving = 2 Fruit exchange

Pictured: Old Fashioned Chicken Pot Pie, Honeydew Mellon Quarters and Blackberries, Quick Tapioca Pudding with Berry Pudding Sauce, p. 79.

Menu Shopping List

Old Fashioned Chicken and Dumplings Menu

Poultry

4		chicken breasts
4		chicken thighs
4		chicken legs --OR--
2		whole fryers

Produce

1	sm	bunch celery
3	lg	carrots
1	lg	head endive lettuce
1	lg	yellow onion
1	sm	red onion
1	sm	bunch parsley
2	med	potatoes
1	pkg	cherry tomatoes

Dairy

1	pint	1% fat cottage cheese, reduced salt
1	doz	eggs (4 eggs required)
1	pint	skim milk

Frozen

1	12oz	can apple juice concentrate
1	12oz	can Mandarin Tangerine juice concentrate
1	12oz	can Mountain Cherry juice concentrate
1	16oz	bag cut green beans

Flours / Powders / Starches

1	sm	container baking powder
1	box	baking soda
1	box	unprocessed bran
1	box	cornstarch
1	sm	bag whole wheat flour

Miscellaneous Groceries
1	sm	box unflavored gelatin
1	sm	container honey
1	sm	bottle lemon juice
1	can	low-fat evaporated milk
1	sm	bottle vegetable oil
1	11oz	can mandarin orange sections (in juice concentrate)
1	sm	jar diced pimentos
1	bottle	Butter Bud Sprinkles

Spices and Seasonings
		salt
1	sm	jar chicken bouillon granules, low sodium
1	bottle	orange peel
1	bottle	lemon peel
1	bottle	Gifford's Basic Spice
1	bottle	Gifford's Dessert Spice
1	bottle	Gifford's Gourmet Spice

To order Gifford's Spices see form in the back of this book.

Instead of Gifford's Spices:

1	bottle	onion powder
1	bottle	garlic powder
1	bottle	ground thyme
1	bottle	white pepper
1	bottle	dill weed
1	bottle	black pepper
1	bottle	ground cinnamon
1	bottle	ground cloves
1	bottle	ground nutmeg
1	bottle	ground allspice
1	bottle	black walnut extract

Remember to check food staples that you already have on hand.

MENU

No Oil Crispy Fried Chicken
Baked Honey Butter Beans
Roasted Corn with Seasoned Bread Crumbs
Chilled Fresh Fruit (your choice)
Blueberries and Cream Turnover

No Oil Crispy Fried Chicken

One of my show-pieces. This recipe should build your confidence and convince you that cooking without oil is easily possible. The taste is un-matched by deep-fried foods.

½	C	whole wheat flour
1	tsp	chicken bouillon granules, low sodium
1	tsp	Gifford's Basic Spice
1	tsp	paprika
¼	C	oat bran
2½	lb	broiler-fryer chicken, cup-up, skin removed and discarded
1	C	chicken broth

Spice Substitute:

Instead of Gifford's Basic Spice, substitute:

1	tsp	beef bouillon granules, low sodium
1	tsp	onion powder
1	tsp	garlic powder
¼	tsp	ground thyme
¼	tsp	white pepper

1. In a blender combine wheat flour, chicken bouillon granules, Basic Spice, paprika, and oat bran; blend until smooth.

2. Rinse chicken pieces; pat dry with a paper towel. Place flour mixture into plastic bag. Add a few chicken pieces at a time; shake

bag to coat chicken. Repeat procedure until all chicken pieces are coated.

3.　　In a large skillet sprayed lightly with a non-stick spray, preheat skillet over medium heat. Add chicken, with meaty pieces toward the center. Prepare a small amount (1 cup) of chicken broth. Using a tablespoon, drop small amounts of broth between and around chicken pieces while browning. Cook uncovered for 15 minutes, turning occasionally to brown evenly. Reduce heat to low. Continue to cook chicken uncovered for 40 minutes, turning occasionally.

Chef's note:　　When I prepare this recipe, I try to get the chicken golden brown in the first 15 minutes of cooking. Occasionally I'll increase the heat to a medium-high setting, which allows more broth to be added to the skillet without making the chicken soggy. Then I'll reduce the temperature to a lower setting and continue with the procedures as I've stated above. Chicken should be golden brown and crispy. The chicken will resemble chicken that has been cooked in oil, with the skin still on it.

Yield: 4 servings

	RCU	FU	Cal	%Fat	P	F	C	Na
Per Serving	0	1	221	19	29	5	16	102

Per Serving = 1 Bread exchange; 3 Meat exchange

Baked Honey Butter Beans

The rich flavor hides that it's only 3% fat. What a treat for us so called "rabbit food eaters" that want to eat healthier foods.

1	29½oz	can kidney beans, lite
½	sm	yellow onion, diced
2	T	Butter Bud Sprinkles
2	tsp	Gifford's Basic Spice
1	T	honey
2	T	apple juice concentrate, unsweetened
½	C	Grape Nuts

Spice Substitute:

Instead of Gifford's Basic Spice, substitute:

1	tsp	chicken bouillon granules, low sodium
2	tsp	onion powder
1	tsp	garlic powder
½	tsp	ground thyme
dash		white pepper

1.   Preheat oven to 350°F.

2.   Combine the chili beans, onions, Butterbud Sprinkles, Basic Spice, honey, and apple juice concentrate in a 9x9x2 inch baking dish that has been sprayed lightly with a non-stick spray. Stir gently to blend. Sprinkle Grape Nuts evenly over bean mixture. Bake for 20 minutes. Serve.

Yield: 4 servings

	RCU	FU	Cal	%Fat	P	F	C	Na
Per Serving	0	0	265	3	13	1	54	739

Per Serving = 1 Fruit exchange; 3 Bread exchange

Roasted Corn with Seasoned Bread Crumbs

1	16oz	bag frozen corn, thawed
2	slices	whole wheat bread, toasted and crumbed
2	tsp	Gifford's Basic Spice
1	lg	egg white, cooked and chopped
1	T	fresh chopped parsley

Spice Substitute:

Instead of Gifford's Basic Spice, substitute:

1	tsp	chicken bouillon granules, low sodium
1	tsp	onion powder
1	tsp	garlic powder
1	tsp	paprika
½	tsp	ground thyme
¼	tsp	ground cloves

Combine spice ingredients in a blender. Blend until smooth, then add to ingredients as called for.

1. Combine all ingredients in a 13x9x2 inch baking dish that has been sprayed lightly with a non-stick spray. Stir gently until blended.

2. Bake in oven at 350°F for 25 to 30 minutes. Serve.

Yield: 4 servings

	RCU	FU	Cal	%Fat	P	F	C	Na
Per Serving	0	0	141	9	6	1	31	80

Per Serving = 2 Bread exchange

Blueberries and Cream Turnover

One busy day at the school, I asked my younger brother, Chef Bill Gifford, to "Create a desert for me!" . Bill was a little surprised at the request but was ready and, as you'll see, these turnovers are absolutely delicious! Thanks Bill.

Dough

1	C	whole wheat flour
¼	C	dry non-fat powdered milk
½	T	Butter Bud Sprinkles
1	tsp	baking soda
¼	C	apple juice concentrate, unsweetened
2	T	non-fat plain yogurt
1	lg	egg white, beaten slightly
¼	C	Grape Nuts

1. In a medium bowl, combine flour, non-fat powdered milk, Butter Buds, baking powder, and baking soda.

2. In a separate bowl, combine the apple juice concentrate, yogurt and egg white. Whisk briskly for 30 seconds. Add liquid mixture to dry ingredients; mix well.

3. Sprinkle a small amount of flour over dough. Roll into a ball. Place dough on a lightly floured surface. Roll dough to ¼ inch thickness. Sprinkle Grape Nuts evenly over dough. Roll lightly to blend Grape Nuts into dough. Using a 4 inch square cutter, cut 8 squares. Turn each square over.

Filling

1	C	frozen blueberries, unsweetened

4. Spread 2 tsp of blueberries evenly in center of each square.

5. Fold dough in half to form triangle. Using a fork dipped in water, seal edges well, pressing with tines of fork. Place turnovers on cookie sheet that has been sprayed lightly with non-stick spray.

6. Bake in preheated oven at 400°F for 15 minutes.

Blueberry Glaze

½	C	apple juice concentrate, unsweetened
½	C	frozen blueberries
2	T	cornstarch mixed together with ½ C water

7. Liquify apple juice concentrate and blueberries in blender.

8. In a small saucepan combine all ingredients. Bring to a boil stirring constantly until mixture thickens.

9. Remove from heat. Brush glaze thoroughly over each baked turnover. Reserve remaining glaze.

Cream Sauce

1	C	1% fat cottage cheese, reduced salt
¼	C	apple juice concentrate, unsweetened
¼	C	reserved blueberry glaze
1	tsp	Gifford's Dessert Spice

Spice Substitute:

Instead of Gifford's Dessert Spice, substitute:

1	tsp	banana flavor extract
½	tsp	almond flavor extract
½	tsp	ground cinnamon
dash		ground cloves

1. Place ingredients into a blender container; blend until smooth. Chill 15 minutes. Spoon over center of turnover when serving.

    Yield: 8 Turnovers

	RCU	FU	Cal	%Fat	P	F	C	Na
Per Turnover	0	0	185	3	8	1	37	232

Per Glazed Turnover with Cream Sauce = 1 Milk exchange; 2½ Fruit exchange; 2 Bread exchange

Menu Shopping List

No Oil Crispy Fried Chicken Menu

Poultry
2½   lb   broiler, fryer chicken

Produce
               Fresh fruit (your choice)
1   sm   yellow onion
1   sm   bunch fresh parsley

Dairy
1   doz   eggs (2 eggs required)
1   sm   container non-fat plain yogurt
1   sm   container 1% fat cottage cheese, reduced salt

Frozen
1   16oz   can apple juice concentrate, unsweetened
1   16oz   bag corn
1   16oz   bag frozen blueberries, unsweetened

Flours / Powders / Starches
1   box   cornstarch
1   sm   bag whole wheat flour
1   sm   box dry non-fat milk powder
1   box   baking soda
1   box   oat bran cereal
1   sm   container baking powder

Miscellaneous Groceries
1   29½oz can chili beans
1   bottle Butter Bud Sprinkles
1   sm   bottle honey
1   sm   box Grape Nuts cereal
1   loaf   whole wheat bread

| 1 | bottle | banana flavor extract |
| 1 | bottle | almond flavor extract |

Spices and Seasonings

1	sm	jar chicken bouillon granules, low sodium
1	bottle	paprika
1	bottle	Gifford's Basic Spice
1	bottle	Gifford's Dessert Spice

To order Gifford's Spices see form in the back of this book.

Instead of Gifford's Spices:

1	sm	jar beef bouillon granules, low sodium
1	bottle	onion powder
1	bottle	garlic powder
1	bottle	thyme
1	bottle	white pepper
1	bottle	ground cinnamon
1	bottle	ground cloves

Remember to check for products you already have on hand.

MENU

Honey Almond Chicken
Ham Fried Rice
Fried Bean Sprouts and Mushrooms
Spicy Chinese Shrimp Salad
Peach Sauce and Halved Cantaloupe with
De-Lites Cream Cheese

Honey Almond Chicken

For some variety and added fun, enjoy this menu in an authentic way. Sit around a coffee table with your shoes off, chop sticks, etc. Wear kimonos if you have them.

4	5oz	chicken breasts, skinless
½	C	Orchard Peach juice concentrate
½	C	water
2	T	honey
1	tsp	Gifford's Chinese Spice
1	tsp	almond flavor extract
2	tsp	cornstarch, mixed with 2 T cold water
1	sm	yellow onion, quartered

Spice Substitute:

Instead of Gifford's Chinese Spice, substitute:

1	tsp	chicken bouillon granules, low sodium
1	tsp	onion powder
½	tsp	ground mustard
½	tsp	ground ginger
⅛	tsp	ground cinnamon
1	tsp	banana extract

1. Preheat oven to 375°F. Arrange chicken breasts in a 13x9x2 inch baking dish.

2. In a saucepan bring to a boil the Orchard Peach juice concentrate, water, honey, Chinese Spice, and almond extract. Add cornstarch mixture slowly stirring constantly until mixture thickens.

3. Pour sauce evenly over chicken breasts. Arrange onion quarters evenly around chicken breasts.

4. Bake for 30 minutes, or until chicken breasts are cooked through. Spoon sauce over chicken when serving.

Yield: 4 servings

	RCU	FU	Cal	%Fat	P	F	C	Na
Per Serving	0	½	279	9	34	3	28	108

Per Serving = 1½ Fruit exchange; 3 Meat exchange

Ham Fried Rice

½	sm	yellow onion, diced
2	oz	turkey-ham, diced
2	lg	egg whites, cooked, chopped
2	T	green onion, diced
1	T	diced pimentos
2	C	cooked brown rice
1	tsp	Gifford's Basic Spice
1	tsp	Gifford's Chinese Spice
¼	tsp	Gifford's Dessert Spice

Spice Substitute:

Instead of the Gifford Spices, substitute:

1	tsp	chicken bouillon granules, low sodium
1	tsp	onion powder
½	tsp	ground ginger
½	tsp	paprika
¼	tsp	ground cloves
⅛	tsp	ground mustard
⅛	tsp	ground fennel
⅛	tsp	ground allspice

1. In a skillet sprayed lightly with a non-stick spray saute the onion, turkey-ham, egg whites, green onion, and pimentos over medium heat until onions are tender.

2. Stir in the cooked rice and spices. Heat through, (about 3 minutes) stirring frequently; serve.

    Yield: 4 servings

	RCU	FU	Cal	%Fat	P	F	C	Na
Per Serving	0	½	402	6	13	3	81	176

Per Serving = 5 Bread exchange; ½ Meat exchange

Fried Bean Sprouts and Mushrooms

½	lb	fresh bean sprouts
6	med	mushrooms, sliced
1	T	lemon juice
1	T	apple juice concentrate, unsweetened
1	tsp	Gifford's Chinese Spice

Spice Substitute:

Instead of Gifford's Chinese Spice, substitute:

1	tsp	onion powder
¼	tsp	cardamon
¼	tsp	ground ginger
⅛	tsp	ground cloves

Mix together in a small dish and use as directed.

1. Spray a large skillet lightly with a non-stick spray. Preheat skillet over medium-high heat.

2. Stir constantly while adding bean sprouts, mushrooms, lemon juice, apple juice concentrate, and Chinese Spice. Stir-fry until mushrooms are tender, about 3 minutes; serve.

Note: If your skillet becomes too hot, remove from heat for a moment or two and then proceed.

Yield: 4 servings

	RCU	FU	Cal	%Fat	P	F	C	Na
Per Serving	0	0	25	7	2	T	5	82

Per Serving = ½ Vegetable exchange

Spicy Chinese Shrimp Salad

8	leaves	red leaf lettuce
8	oz	cooked baby shrimp
2	sm	tomatoes, one sliced, one chopped
1	med	celery stalk, diced
3	T	tomato puree
2	tsp	Orchard Peach juice concentrate
1	tsp	lemon juice
1	tsp	lime juice
1	tsp	prepared horseradish
1	tsp	chicken bouillon granules, low sodium
1	tsp	Gifford's Chinese Spice
		lemon slices to garnish

Spice Substitute:

Instead of Gifford's Chinese Spice, substitute:

1	tsp	chicken bouillon granules, , low sodium, additional
1	tsp	onion powder
½	tsp	ground ginger
½	tsp	ground mustard
½	tsp	ground cardamon
⅛	tsp	ground cloves

1. Arrange 2 leaves red leaf lettuce onto each of 4 salad plates.

2. Combine remaining ingredients in a mixing bowl; stir well to blend. Cover and chill a few minutes.

3. Spoon shrimp salad over lettuce. Garnish with lemon slices.

    Yield: 4 servings

	RCU	FU	Cal	%Fat	P	F	C	Na
Per Serving	0	0	97	14	13	2	8	110

Per Serving = ½ Vegetable exchange; 1 Meat exchange

Peach Sauce and Halved Cantaloupe with De-Lites Cream Cheese

½	C	De-Lites Cream Cheese (see recipe on page 14)
2	sm	ripe cantaloupes, halved, seeds and membrane removed
1	16oz	bag frozen peach slices, thawed, juice reserved
2	T	cornstarch
¼	C	pineapple juice concentrate
1	tsp	Gifford's Dessert Spice
1	tsp	dried orange peel
⅓	C	orange juice

Spice Substitute:

Instead of Gifford's Dessert Spice, substitute:

2	tsp	Butter Bud Sprinkles
½	tsp	ground cinnamon
1	tsp	banana extract

1. Coarsely chop half of the sliced peaches; set aside.

2. In a saucepan combine reserved peach juice, cornstarch, and pineapple juice concentrate; whisk gently to blend. Cook mixture over medium heat, stirring constantly until thick and bubbly; remove from heat.

3. Stir in Dessert Spice, orange peel, chopped peaches, and orange juice; cover and chill a few minutes.

4. Place cantaloupe halves on 4 dessert dishes. Place remaining peach slices evenly in cantaloupe halves. Spoon peach sauce over peaches in cantaloupe halves. Top off with a dollop of cream cheese; serve.

Yield: 4 servings

	RCU	FU	Cal	%Fat	P	F	C	Na
Per Serving	0	0	181	6	7	1	39	143

Per Serving = 2 Fruit exchange

Menu Shopping List

Honey Almond Chicken Menu

Poultry / Seafood
4	5oz	skinless chicken breasts
1	sm	turkey-ham roll
8	oz	cooked baby shrimp

Produce
2	sm	yellow onions
1	sm	bunch green onions
8	oz	fresh bean sprouts
6	med	mushrooms
1	head	red leaf lettuce
2	sm	tomatoes
1	sm	bunch celery
1	sm	lemon
2	sm	ripe cantaloupes

Dairy
1	pint	1% fat cottage cheese, reduced salt
1	doz	eggs(2 eggs required)

Frozen
1	12oz	can pineapple juice concentrate
1	12oz	can apple juice concentrate
1	12oz	can Orchard Peach juice concentrate
1	16oz	bag frozen peach slices, unsweetened
1	sm	can orange juice concentrate

Flours / Powders / Starches
1	box	cornstarch

Miscellaneous Groceries
1	bottle	honey
1	bottle	almond flavor extract

1	sm	bag long grain brown rice
1	sm	jar diced pimentos
1	sm	bottle lemon juice
1	sm	bottle lime juice
1	sm	can tomato puree
1	sm	jar prepared horseradish
1	bottle	vanilla

Spices and Seasonings

1	sm	jar chicken bouillon granules, low sodium
1	bottle	orange peel
1	bottle	Gifford's Chinese Spice
1	bottle	Gifford's Basic Spice
1	bottle	Gifford's Dessert Spice

To order Gifford's Spices see form in the back of the book.

Instead of Gifford's Spices:

1	bottle	onion powder
1	bottle	ground mustard
1	bottle	ground ginger
1	bottle	paprika
1	bottle	ground clove
1	bottle	ground fennel
1	bottle	ground allspice
1	bottle	ground cardamon
1	bottle	ground cinnamon
1	bottle	banana extract

Remember to check for products that you already have at home.

MENU

Fried Chicken Steak with Country Gravy
Potatoes O'Brien
Steamed Crinkle Cut Carrots in Pineapple Juice
Crisp Apple Crunch Dessert

Fried Chicken Steak with Country Gravy

4	5oz	chicken breasts, boneless, skinless
1	C	chicken broth, low sodium, set aside

Mix together:

½	C	whole wheat flour
1	T	Gifford's Basic Spice
1	tsp	onion powder

Spice Substitute:

Instead of Gifford's Basic Spice, substitute:

2	tsp	chicken bouillon granules
2	tsp	onion powder
1	tsp	garlic powder
½	tsp	ground thyme

1.   Coat each chicken breast thoroughly with flour mixture.

2.   Preheat a non-stick skillet over medium-high heat. Place floured chicken breasts in skillet. Using a tablespoon, occasionally pour chicken broth around and between breasts while browning.

3.   When chicken is golden brown on one side, turn breasts over and repeat procedure. Reduce heat to low and cook chicken 15 minutes longer until cooked through, turning occasionally.

Gravy

1	C	water
1½	tsp	Gifford's Basic Spice
1½	tsp	chicken bouillon granules, low sodium
½	tsp	ground caraway seed, optional
½	tsp	sage, rubbed or ground
1	tsp	cornstarch, mixed with 3 T cold water
1	C	low-fat evaporated milk

Spice Substitute:

Instead of Gifford's Basic Spice, substitute:

1½	T	onion powder

4. In a saucepan combine the water, Basic Spice or onion powder, chicken bouillon, caraway, and sage. Bring to a boil.

5. Add cornstarch mixture slowly; stir constantly until mixture thickens.

6. Reduce heat; add milk. Stir to blend and simmer 5 minutes. Spoon over fried chicken steaks when serving.

    Gravy yields: approx. 2 cups

    Yield: 4 servings

	RCU	FU	Cal	%Fat	P	F	C	Na
Per ½ Cup	0	½	315	11	44	4	25	179

Per ½ Cup = ½ Milk exchange; 1 Bread exchange; 3 Meat exchange

Potatoes O'Brien

I'm asked frequently, "What do you eat the most at home?" Well, at home I'm pretty plain. This recipe, along with a piece of chicken, satisfies my palate--2 to 3 times a week. My only problem though is that I like these potatoes so much, I eat all 4 servings. Oh well!

2	med	potatoes, diced
1	C	chicken broth, low sodium
½	sm	yellow onion, diced
1	sm	bell pepper, diced
1	T	pimentos, diced
1	T	Gifford's Basic Spice

Spice Substitute:

Instead of Gifford's Basic Spice, substitute:

2	tsp	beef bouillon granules, low sodium, blended to a powder
1	tsp	onion powder
1	tsp	garlic powder
1	tsp	paprika
½	tsp	thyme
¼	tsp	black pepper

1. In a skillet sprayed lightly with a non-stick spray, cook potatoes in the chicken broth until they are tender, stirring frequently.

2. Add onions and bell peppers, stir to blend. Fry potatoes, onion, and bell peppers stirring frequently until potatoes are browned and vegetables are tender. Broth will evaporate while potatoes are cooking. Add pimentos and Basic Spice. Stir and serve.

Yield: 4 servings

	RCU	FU	Cal	%Fat	P	F	C	Na
Per Serving	0	0	54	17	4	1	7	9

Per Serving = ½ Vegetable exchange

Steamed Crinkle Cut Carrots in Pineapple Juice

1	16oz	bag frozen crinkles cut carrots
1	C	water
¼	C	pineapple juice concentrate
1	tsp	Gifford's Dessert Spice
1	tsp	banana flavor extract
1	tsp	dried orange peel
½	tsp	ground cinnamon

1. In a saucepan combine all ingredients; stir and bring to a boil.

2. Reduce heat; simmer for 8 to 10 minutes. Remove from heat. Drain and serve.

   Yield: 4 servings

	RCU	FU	Cal	%Fat	P	F	C	Na
Per Serving	0	0	82	3	2	T	19	68

Per Serving = ½ Fruit exchange; 1½ Vegetable exchange

Crisp Apple Crunch Dessert

1	lg	red delicious apple
¼	C	apple juice concentrate, unsweetened
½	C	raisins
1	tsp	Gifford's Dessert Spice
½	C	Grape Nuts
½	C	De-lites cream cheese, optional (see recipe on page 13)

Spice Substitute:

Instead of Gifford's Dessert Spice, substitute:

½	tsp	ground cinnamon
¼	tsp	allspice
⅛	tsp	ground cloves

1. Remove core and dice apple.

2. In a skillet sprayed lightly with a non-stick spray cook diced apple over medium-heat until tender.

3. Add apple juice concentrate, raisins, Dessert Spice and Grape-nuts; stir and serve. Top off each serving with a dollop of De-Lites Cream Cheese, if desired.

    Yield: 4 servings

	RCU	FU	Cal	%Fat	P	F	C	Na
Per Serving	0	0	168	2	3	T	42	107

Per Serving = 2 Fruit exchange; ½ Bread exchange

Menu Shopping List

Fried Chicken Steak Menu

Poultry
4	5oz	boneless, skinless, chicken breasts

Produce
2	med	potatoes
1	sm	yellow onion
1	sm	bell pepper
1	lg	red delicious apple

Frozen
1	16oz	bag crinkle cut carrots
1	12oz	can pineapple juice concentrate
1	12oz	can apple juice concentrate

Flours / Powders / Starches
1	sm	bag whole wheat flour
1	box	cornstarch
1	sm	box Grape Nuts cereal

Miscellaneous Groceries
1	can	low-fat evaporated milk
1	sm	jar pimentos (diced)
1	sm	box raisins
1	bottle	banana flavor extract

Spices and Seasonings
1	sm	jar chicken bouillon granules, low sodium
1	bottle	ground caraway seed
1	bottle	onion powder
1	bottle	rubbed sage
1	bottle	Gifford's Basic Spice
1	bottle	Gifford's Dessert Spice

To order Gifford's Spices see form in the back of this book.

Instead of Gifford's Spices:

1	bottle	garlic powder
1	bottle	thyme
1	bottle	paprika
1	bottle	black pepper
1	bottle	ground cinnamon
1	bottle	ground cloves
1	bottle	ground allspice

Remember to check products you have on hand.

MENU

Old Fashioned Chicken Pot Pie
Honeydew Melon Quarters and Blackberries
Quick Tapioca Pudding with
Berry Pudding Sauce

Old Fashioned Chicken Pot Pie

This is the menu I picked for the front cover of the cookbook. What more can I say? Enjoy!

½	lb	chicken breast tenders, cubed
1	sm	onion, diced
1	med	celery stalk, diced
1	med	carrot, diced
4	med	mushrooms, quartered
2	C	frozen garden peas
1	C	water
2	T	Butter Bud Sprinkles
2	tsp	Gifford's Basic Spice
1	tsp	chicken bouillon granules, low sodium
1	tsp	ground mustard
pinch		Gifford's Gourmet Spice
2	T	cornstarch, mixed with ⅓ C cold water
1	C	low-fat evaporated milk

Spice Substitute:

Instead of Gifford's Basic and Gourmet Spice, substitute:

2	tsp	chicken bouillon granules, low sodium
2	tsp	onion powder
1	tsp	garlic powder
½	tsp	thyme
dash		white pepper

1. In a large saucepan sprayed lightly with a non-stick spray combine the chicken, onion, celery, and carrots, saute over medium-high heat until chicken is cooked through. Stirring occasionally, (about 5 minutes).

2. Add the mushrooms, peas, and water. Stir to blend.

3. Add Butter Bud Sprinkles, Basic Spice, chicken granules, ground mustard, and Gourmet Spice. Stir. Bring to a boil.

4. Slowly add cornstarch mixture and stir constantly until thick. Reduce heat at once.

5. Add milk. Stir. Cook on low heat 5 minutes. Remove from heat. Cover and set aside.

Pot Pie Crust

⅔	C	whole wheat flour
⅓	C	oat bran
1	tsp	baking powder
¼	tsp	salt
2	lg	egg whites, slightly beaten
1	tsp	vegetable oil
¼	C	skim milk
2	T	Orchard Peach juice concentrate

6. In a mixing bowl combine the whole wheat flour, oat bran, baking powder, and salt. Stir to blend.

7. In a separate bowl combine the egg whites, oil, skim milk, and Orchard Peach concentrate. Stir to blend.

8. Add to flour mixture stirring with a fork until combined. Turn dough onto a well floured surface. Knead dough until smooth. Cover, and let rest for 10 minutes.

9. Roll dough on floured surface until smooth and about ¼ inch thick. Cut dough into four 5-inch circles.

10. Spoon chicken mixture into 4 casserole dishes. Place pie crust circles over each dish, flute edges. Cut slits in top for excape of steam. Bake

in oven at 450°F for 10 to 12 minutes, or until golden brown.

Yield: 4 pot pies

	RCU	FU	Cal	%Fat	P	F	C	Na
Per Pot Pie	0	½	331	11	28	4	47	408

Per Pot Pie = ½ Milk exchange; 1 Vegetable exchange; 2 Bread exchange; 1½ Meat exchange

Honeydew Melon Quarters and Blackberries

8	leaves	red leaf lettuce
1	sm	honeydew melon, quartered
2	C	frozen blackberries, thawed
		Gifford's Dessert Spice to taste
		orange slices to garnish, if desired

1. Arrange 2 red leaf lettuce leaves onto each of 4 salad plates. Place 1 quarter honeydew melon over leaves.

2. Spoon ½ C blackberries around each melon quarter. Sprinkle Dessert Spice over top. Garnish with orange slices. Serve.

Yield: 4 servings

	RCU	FU	Cal	%Fat	P	F	C	Na
Per Serving	0	0	165	4	3	1	42	35

Per Serving = 2½ Fruit exchange

Quick Tapioca Pudding

3	T	quick cooking tapioca
2	lg	egg whites, slightly beaten
¾	C	Orchard Peach juice concentrate
2¼	C	skim milk
½	tsp	vanilla
1	tsp	Gifford's Dessert Spice

Spice Substitute:

Instead of Gifford's Dessert Spice, substitute:

| ½ | tsp | ground cinnamon |

1. Combine the tapioca, egg whites, and Orchard Peach concentrate in a saucepan. Slowly pour in milk. Stir to blend. Let mixture stand for 5 minutes.

2. Bring to a boil stirring constantly. Remove from heat. Stir in vanilla and Dessert Spice.

3. Pour into 4 dessert dishes. Let stand at room temperature for 15 minutes, then stir once and chill until firm.

Yield: 4 servings

	RCU	FU	Cal	%Fat	P	F	C	Na
Per Serving	0	0	173	3	7	T	36	103

Per Serving = ½ Milk exchange; 1½ Fruit exchange

Berry Pudding Sauce

1	C	frozen boysenberries, thawed
½	C	Mountain Cherry juice concentrate
1	tsp	cherry flavor extract
1	T	Butter Bud Sprinkles
1	tsp	Gifford's Dessert Spice
1	T	cornstarch, mixed with 3 T cold water

Spice Substitute:

Instead of Gifford's Dessert Spice, substitute:

1	tsp	banana flavor extract
½	tsp	black walnut extract
½	tsp	ground cinnamon
⅛	tsp	ground cloves

1. Combine the boysenberries, Mountain Cherry juice concentrate, cherry flavor extract, Butter Bud Sprinkles, and Dessert Spice in saucepan. Bring to a boil. Reduce heat.

2. Slowly add cornstarch mixture and stir constantly until sauce thickens. Remove from heat. Spoon over tapioca pudding when serving.

   Yield: 6 (¼ C) servings ; approx. 1½ cups sauce

	RCU	FU	Cal	%Fat	P	F	C	Na
Per ¼ Cup	0	0	93	2	1	T	22	10

Per ¼ Cup = 1 Fruit exchange

Menu Shopping List

Old Fashioned Chicken Pot Pie Menu

Poultry
	8oz	chicken tenders

Produce
1	sm	yellow onion
1	sm	bunch celery
1	med	carrot
4	med	mushrooms
1	sm	honeydew melon
1	head	red leaf lettuce
1	sm	orange

Dairy
1	doz	eggs (4 eggs required)
1	quart	skim milk

Frozen
1	16oz	bag frozen blackberries
1	12oz	can Orchard Peach juice concentrate
1	12oz	can Mountain Cherry juice concentrate
1	bag	frozen peas

Flours / Powders / Starches
1	sm	bag whole wheat flour
1	box	oat bran
1	sm	container baking powder
1	box	cornstarch

Pictured: De-Lites Chicken Picante, Spanish Corn Rice Pilaf, Baked Bean Tortilla Chip, Pineapple-Oregano Zucchini, and De-Licious Bread Pudding, p.94.

Miscellaneous Groceries

1	bottle	Butter Bud Sprinkles
1	can	low-fat evaporated milk
1	sm	container vegetable oil
1	box	quick tapioca
1	bottle	vanilla
1	bottle	cherry flavor extract
1	bottle	banana flavor extract (optional)
1	bottle	black walnut extract (optional)

Spices and Seasonings

1	jar	chicken bouillon granules, low sodium
1	bottle	(dry) ground mustard
	bottle	salt
1	bottle	Gifford's Basic Spice
1	bottle	Gifford's Gourmet Spice
1	bottle	Gifford's Dessert Spice

To order Gifford's Spices see form in the back of this book.

Instead of Gifford's Spices:

1	bottle	onion powder
1	bottle	garlic powder
1	bottle	thyme
1	bottle	white pepper
1	bottle	ground cinnamon
1	bottle	ground cloves

Remember to check for products that you already have on hand.

Pictured: De-Licious Eggs Benedict, Golden Hashbrown Potatoes, A Special Orange Juice, Chilled Fresh Fruit, De-Lites Hot Bran Muffins and Sweet Berry Preserves, p. 121.

MENU

Roast Chicken with Plum Sauce
Hot Fruit Medley with Crinkle Cut Carrots
De-Lites Basic Spice Rice Pilaf
Sweet Spiced Oat Bran Muffins
Bubbly Blackberry Cobbler

Roast Chicken with Plum Sauce

Every holiday season I try to come up with some different, but very colorful recipes. I introduced this menu in front of 275 people who also had this for dinner. They did not know before hand that this was low-fat. Surprise! They loved it.

2		whole fryer chickens, remove skin and discard wings, neck, and giblets
1	med	orange, cut in half
2	17oz	cans purple plums, drained and pitted
½	C	water
¼	C	apple-raspberry juice concentrate, unsweetened
1	tsp	Gifford's Chinese Spice
1	tsp	Gifford's Dessert Spice
1	clove	garlic, minced
2	tsp	paprika

Spice Substitute:

Instead of Gifford's Chinese and Dessert Spice, substitute:

1	tsp	chicken bouillon granules, low sodium
1	tsp	onion powder
1	tsp	ground mustard
½	tsp	ground cinnamon
¼	tsp	ground nutmeg

1.   Pre-heat oven to 375°F.

2.   Place whole fryers in a large baking dish. Put ½ orange inside cavity of each fryer.

3.   Combine remaining ingredients in a blender. Blend ingredients until smooth, about 1 minute.

4.   Pour plum sauce evenly over fryers. Bake uncovered for 40 to 45 minutes.

Yield: 6 servings

	RCU	FU	Cal	%Fat	P	F	C	Na
Per Serving	0	1	301	14	32	5	33	180

Per Serving = 2 Fruit exchange; 3 Meat exchange

Hot Fruit Medley with Crinkle Cut Carrots

1	16oz	bag Fruit Medley
1	16oz	bag frozen crinkle cut carrots

5.   Mix the Fruit Medley and carrots together in a bowl.

6.   Add to baking dish with chicken at the 20 minute mark of the cooking time. Stir to blend with plum sauce around each fryer.

7.   For serving, place the chicken sauce, fruit, and carrots on a large platter. Serve buffet style if desired, or cut desired pieces from the chicken for each serving and spoon sauce, fruit, and carrots onto each serving plate.

Yield: 6 servings

	RCU	FU	Cal	%Fat	P	F	C	Na
Per Serving	0	0	54	6	2	T	13	68

Per Serving = ½ Fruit exchange; 1 Vegetable exchange

De-Lites Basic Spice Rice Pilaf

2½	C	water
2	tsp	Gifford's Basic Spice
½	tsp	paprika
1	C	long grain brown rice

Spice Substitute:

Instead of Gifford's Basic Spice, substitute:

2	tsp	chicken bouillon granules, low sodium
2	tsp	onion powder
1	tsp	garlic powder
½	tsp	ground thyme

1. Bring the water and spices to a boil in a saucepan.

2. Stir in the rice. Reduce heat to low. Cover pan tightly.

3. Cook rice for 30 minutes. Do not remove cover.

4. Remove from heat. Let rice stand covered for an additional 20 minutes. Remove cover. Gently fluff rice with a fork, starting at the top and working your way to the bottom of pan. Serve.

Yield: 4 to 6 servings

	RCU	FU	Cal	%Fat	P	F	C	Na
Per Serving	0	0	121	5	3	T	26	3

Per Serving = 1½ Bread exchange

Sweet Spiced Oat Bran Muffins

2¼	C	oat bran
2	tsp	baking powder
½	tsp	baking soda
¼	tsp	salt
2	lg	egg whites, slightly beaten

¾	C	low-fat evaporated milk
⅔	C	Orchard Peach juice concentrate
2	T	honey
2½	tsp	vegetable oil
¼	tsp	almond extract
1	tsp	Gifford's Dessert Spice

Spice Substitute:

Instead of Gifford's Dessert Spice, substitute:

¾	tsp	almond extract, additional
½	tsp	black walnut extract
½	tsp	banana flavor extract
½	tsp	ground cinnamon
¼	tsp	ground cloves
⅛	tsp	allspice

1. Pre-heat oven to 400°F. Spray a teflon muffin pan lightly with a non-stick spray.

2. Combine dry ingredients in a bowl; stir to blend. Make a well in center of bran mixture.

3. Add remaining ingredients to well. Stir gently to blend, careful to not over mix.

4. Fill each muffin cup almost to the top. Bake for 15 to 18 minutes, or until golden brown.

   Yield: 12 muffins

	RCU	FU	Cal	%Fat	P	F	C	Na
Per Muffin	0	0	116	18	5	2	21	227

Per Muffin = ½ Fruit exchange; ½ Bread exchange

Bubbly Blackberry Cobbler

1	C	water
½	C	Mountain Cherry juice concentrate
2	T	Butter Bud Sprinkles
1½	tsp	Gifford's Dessert Spice
½	tsp	vanilla
½	tsp	black walnut extract
1	16oz	bag frozen blackberries, thawed
2	T	cornstarch, mixed with ⅓ C cold water

Spice Substitute:

Instead of Gifford's Dessert Spice, substitute:

1	tsp	cherry flavor extract
1	tsp	strawberry flavor extract
½	tsp	ground cinnamon

1. In a saucepan combine water, Mountain Cherry juice concentrate, Butter Buds, Dessert Spice, vanilla, blackberry extract, and half of the blackberries. Bring mixture to a boil.

2. Slowly add cornstarch mixture and stir constantly until mixture thickens. Remove from heat.

3. Fold remaining blackberries into mixture. Pour into small baking dish.

Cobbler Dough

⅔	C	whole wheat flour
⅓	C	oat bran
2	tsp	baking powder
dash		salt
2	lg	egg whites, slightly beaten
3	T	skim milk
3	T	Orchard Peach juice concentrate
1	tsp	vegetable oil
		De-Lites cream cheese, optional (see recipe on page 14)

4. In a bowl combine the whole wheat flour, oat bran, baking powder, and salt. Stir to blend.

5. In a separate bowl combine the egg whites, skim milk, Orchard Peach concentrate, milk, and oil. Stir to blend. Add to flour mixture stirring with a fork until combined. Do not over mix.

6. Use a tablespoon to evenly drop dough directly onto blackberry mixture. Cover. Bake in a 375°F oven for 20 to 25 minutes. Serve.

Note: Top off with a teaspoon of De-Lites Cream Cheese if desired.

Yield: 4 servings

	RCU	FU	Cal	%Fat	P	F	C	Na
Per Serving	0	½	294	8	8	3	62	247

Per Serving = 2½ Fruit exchange; 1 Bread exchange

Menu Shopping List

Roast Chicken with Plum Sauce Menu

Poultry
2   whole fryer chickens

Produce
1   orange
1   sm   bud garlic

Dairy
1   pint   skim milk
1   doz   eggs (4 eggs required)

Frozen
1   12oz   can apple-raspberry juice concentrate
1   12oz   can Mountain Cherry juice concentrate
1   12oz   can Orchard Peach juice concentrate
1   16oz   bag crinkle cut carrots
1   16oz   bag Fruit Medley
1   16oz   bag frozen blackberries

Flours / Powders / Starches
1   box   oat bran
1   sm   bag whole wheat flour
1   box   cornstarch
1   sm   container baking powder
1   box   baking soda

Miscellaneous Groceries
2   17oz   cans purple plums
1   bag   long grain brown rice
1   can   low-fat evaporated milk
1   sm   bottle honey
1   sm   bottle vegetable oil
1   bottle   Butter Bud Sprinkles

1   bottle   vanilla
1   bottle   almond flavor extract
1   bottle   black walnut extract

Spices and Seasonings

1   bottle   paprika
1   bottle   Gifford's Chinese Spice
1   bottle   Gifford's Dessert Spice
1   bottle   Gifford's Basic Spice
                    salt

To order Gifford's Spices see form in the back of this book.

Instead of Gifford's Spices:

1   bottle   chicken bouillon granules, low sodium
1   bottle   onion powder
1   bottle   garlic powder
1   bottle   ground mustard
1   bottle   ground cinnamon
1   bottle   ground nutmeg
1   bottle   thyme
1   bottle   ground cloves
1   bottle   ground allspice
1   bottle   banana flavor extract
1   bottle   cherry flavor extract --or--
1   bottle   strawberry flavor extract

Remember to check food staples on hand.

MENU

De-Lites Chicken Picante
Spanish Corn Rice Pilaf
Baked Bean Tortilla Chips
Pineapple-Oregano Zucchini
De-Licious Bread Pudding

De-Lites Chicken Picante

4	5oz	chicken breasts, boneless, skinless
1	med	tomato, peeled, quartered
2	med	celery stalks, quartered
1	sm	onion, quartered
½	sm	bell pepper, cut-up
3	T	pineapple juice concentrate
½	C	tomato puree
2	tsp	Gifford's Mexican Spice
1	tsp	lemon juice
1	tsp	lime juice

Spice Substitute:

Instead of Gifford's Mexican Spice, substitute:

2	tsp	chicken bouillon granules, low sodium
2	tsp	onion powder
1	tsp	garlic powder
1	tsp	chili powder
½	tsp	ground cumin
½	tsp	oregano
¼	tsp	ground cloves

1. Place chicken breasts in a 13x9x2 baking dish that has been sprayed lightly with a non-stick spray.

2.   In a blender, or food processor, combine remaining ingredients. On chop speed, blend until minced. Pour sauce evenly over chicken breasts.

3.   Bake in a 375°F oven 35 to 40 minutes. Serve.

Yield: 4 servings

	RCU	FU	Cal	%Fat	P	F	C	Na
Per Serving	0	½	239	11	35	3	18	237

Per Serving = 1 Vegetable exchange; 3 Meat exchange

Spanish Corn Rice Pilaf

2½	C	water
1	C	brown rice
1	tsp	chicken bouillon granules, low sodium
2	tsp	Gifford's Mexican Spice
1	C	frozen corn, thawed
1	T	snipped parsley

Spice Substitute:

Instead of Gifford's Mexican Spice, substitute:

1	tsp	beef bouillon granules, low sodium
1	tsp	onion powder
1	tsp	garlic powder
2	tsp	chili powder
½	tsp	ground nutmeg
¼	tsp	ground cinnamon

1.   In a saucepan combine water, chicken bouillon granules, and Mexican Spice. Bring to a boil.

2.   Add brown rice and corn. Stir to blend. Cover tightly.

3.   Reduce heat to low and cook 30 minutes. Do not remove cover. Remove from heat.

4.   With cover still on, let pilaf stand for 15 additional minutes. Remove cover. Gently fluff while adding parsley. Serve.

Yield: 6 servings

	RCU	FU	Cal	%Fat	P	F	C	Na
Per Serving	0	0	155	7	4	1	33	237

Per Serving = 2 Bread exchange

Baked Bean Tortilla Chips

As a snack this recipe is terrific. They also freeze well.

4		corn tortillas
2	15oz	cans pinto beans, without sugar, drained
1	tsp	chicken bouillon granules, low sodium
1	tsp	Gifford's Mexican Spice
		pepper to taste
½	C	mozzarella cheese, finely grated

Spice Substitute:

Instead of Gifford's Mexican Spice, substitute:

2	tsp	onion powder
1	tsp	garlic powder
½	tsp	chili powder

1.   Cut corn tortillas into six pie-shaped wedges.

2.   In a blender combine the pinto beans, bouillon, and spices. Blend until smooth.

3.   Spray a cookie sheet lightly with a non-stick spray. Lay out cut tortillas evenly on sheet. Spoon bean mixture onto each tortilla. Sprinkle cheese over the beans.

4.   Bake in a 350°F oven 15 minutes, or until golden brown. Serve.

Yield: 4 servings

	RCU	FU	Cal	%Fat	P	F	C	Na
Per Serving	0	2	449	14	29	7	70	212

Per Serving = 5 Bread exchange; 2½ Meat exchange; ½ Fat exchange

Pineapple-Oregano Zucchini

They say that some of the simpler things are the best. Here is one vegetable dish that proves it. I've always enjoyed how the ingredients blend together so well.

1	lg	zucchini squash, sliced
1	sm	pineapple chunks, drained
1	tsp	oregano
		pepper to taste

1. In a skillet sprayed lightly with a non-stick spray, saute zucchini squash over medium-high heat until squash begins to brown.

2. Add pineapple chunks to skillet. Stir to blend.

3. Add oregano and pepper. Stir and serve.

   Yield: 4 servings

	RCU	FU	Cal	%Fat	P	F	C	Na
Per Serving	0	0	53	2	1	T	14	3

Per Serving = ½ Fruit exchange; ½ Vegetable exchange

De-Licious Bread Pudding

1	box	oat bran graham crackers
6	slices	whole wheat bread, torn into small pieces
½	C	currants
1	med	banana
2	C	low-fat evaporated milk
2	lg	egg whites, slightly beaten
¼	C	apple juice concentrate, unsweetened
¼	C	Orchard Peach juice concentrate
1	T	honey
1	tsp	vanilla
1	T	Butter Bud Sprinkles
2	tsp	Gifford's Dessert Spice

Spice Substitute:

Instead of Gifford's Dessert Spice, substitute:

1½	tsp	ground cinnamon
½	tsp	ground allspice
½	tsp	ground cloves
¼	tsp	ground nutmeg

1. Lay out graham crackers in a baking dish. Spread bread pieces over crackers evenly. Sprinkle currants evenly over bread.

2. Mix remaining ingredients together in a mixing bowl. Stir to blend. Pour milk mixture evenly over bread mixture.

3. Bake in a 375°F oven for 25 minutes, or until golden brown on top. Serve.

Yield: 8 servings

	RCU	FU	Cal	%Fat	P	F	C	Na
Per Serving	0	½	313	12	11	4	62	422

Per Serving = ½ Milk exchange; 1 Fruit exchange; 2 Bread exchange; ½ Fat exchange

Menu Shopping List

De-Lites Chicken Picante Menu

Poultry
4	5oz	skinless, boneless chicken breasts

Produce
1	sm	tomato
1	sm	bunch celery
1	sm	onion
1	sm	bell pepper
1	sm	bunch fresh parsley
1	lg	zucchini squash
1	med	banana

Dairy
4	oz	bag shredded mozzarella cheese
1	doz	eggs (2 eggs required)

Frozen
1	12oz	can pineapple juice concentrate
1	12oz	can Orchard Peach juice concentrate
1	bag	frozen corn

Miscellaneous Groceries
1	sm	can tomato puree
1	sm	bottle lemon juice
1	sm	bottle lime juice
1	sm	bag long grain brown rice
2	15oz	cans pinto beans, without sugar
1	sm	can low-fat evaporated milk
1	sm	bottle honey
1	sm	bottle vanilla
1	loaf	whole grain bread
1	box	oat bran graham crackers

1	sm	box raisins
1	sm	can pineapple chunks

Spices and Seasonings

1	jar	chicken bouillon granules, low sodium
1	bottle	oregano
	bottle	black pepper
1	bottle	Gifford's Mexican Spice
1	bottle	Gifford's Dessert Spice

To order Gifford's Spices see form in the back of this book.

Instead of Gifford's Spices:

1	bottle	onion powder
1	bottle	garlic powder
1	bottle	chili powder
1	bottle	ground cloves
1	bottle	ground nutmeg
1	bottle	ground cinnamon
1	bottle	ground allspice

Check products on hand before going to the store.

MENU

De-Lites Gourmet Chicken
Gourmet Spice Rice Pilaf
Steamed Asparagus with
A Spicy Mustard Sauce
Yeast Free Wheat Bread
L'Orange and Sherry Sauce

De-Lites Gourmet Chicken

1	lb	chicken breast tenders
1	C	water
1	T	cornstarch, mixed with 3 T cold water
3	T	low-fat evaporated milk
2	tsp	Gifford's Gourmet Spice
1½	tsp	chicken bouillon granules, low sodium
2	T	pineapple juice concentrate

Spice Substitute:

Instead of Gifford's Gourmet Spice, substitute:

½	tsp	chicken bouillon granules, low sodium, additional
1	tsp	onion powder
1	tsp	garlic powder
1	tsp	dill weed
1	tsp	tarragon leaves, (crushed)
¼	tsp	ground fennel seed
⅛	tsp	ground cardamon

1. Place chicken breast tenders in a 13x9x2 inch baking dish that has been sprayed lightly with a non-stick spray.

2.   In a saucepan bring water to a boil. Slowly add cornstarch mixture and stir constantly until thick. Reduce heat.

3.   Add remaining ingredients. Stir to blend. Simmer 5 minutes.

4.   Pour sauce over chicken tenders. Bake in 350°F oven 25 min. Serve.

Yield: 4 (4 oz) servings

	RCU	FU	Cal	%Fat	P	F	C	Na
Per Serving	0	0	174	11	28	2	9	95

Per Serving = 2 Meat exchange

Gourmet Spice Rice Pilaf

2½	C	water
½	sm	yellow onion, finely diced
2	T	Butter Bud Sprinkles
2	tsp	paprika
1	tsp	Gifford's Gourmet Spice
1	tsp	beef bouillon granules, low sodium
1	C	brown rice

Spice Substitute:

Instead of Gifford's Gourmet Spice, substitute:

1	tsp	onion powder
1	tsp	garlic powder
1	tsp	dill weed
½	tsp	cardamon
¼	tsp	white pepper
¼	tsp	ground fennel seed

1.   In a saucepan bring water, onion, Butter Bud Sprinkles, paprika, Gourmet Spice, and beef bouillon granules to a boil.

2.   Stir in rice. Return to a boil. Reduce heat to low and cover pan tightly. Cook rice for 3 minutes.

3.   Remove from heat. Let rice stand with cover still on tightly for 5 minutes.

4.   Remove cover. Fluff rice gently with a fork before serving. Serve.

Yield: 4 to 6 servings

	RCU	FU	Cal	%Fat	P	F	C	Na
Per Serving	0	0	133	6	3	1	28	148

Per Serving = 1½ Bread exchange

Steamed Asparagus with a Spicy Mustard Sauce
Steamed Asparagus

	Asparagus, desired amount, fresh or frozen
	water
dash	salt

1.   Remove woody bases from asparagus stalks. The best way to do this is by holding the stalk in both hands and bending. The stalk will snap easily where the tender part begins.

2.   Add a dash of salt to 1-inch of water in saucepan. Bring water to a boil. Add asparagus stalks to boiling water, standing them upright in the pan. Cover and cook 12 minutes.

Note: The above procedure is for fresh asparagus. If using frozen asparagus, follow directions on package.

Spicy Mustard Sauce

1	C	De-Lites Cream Cheese (see recipe on page 14)
1	T	Dijon mustard
½	tsp	Gifford's Mexican Spice
¼	tsp	white pepper

Spice Substitute:

Instead of Gifford's Gourmet Spice, substitute:

½	tsp	chicken bouillon granules, low sodium
½	tsp	onion powder
½	tsp	chili powder
⅛	tsp	red cayenne pepper
		omit the white pepper

3. In a small mixing bowl, gently mix ingredients together. Spoon 2 oz. of sauce over each serving of asparagus.

Serving size asparagus ½ cup

Sauce yields: 1¼ cup

	RCU	FU	Cal	%Fat	P	F	C	Na
Per Serving	0	0	81	13	11	1	9	189

Per Serving = 1 Vegetable Exchange

Yeast Free Wheat Bread

2¼	C	whole wheat flour
½	C	unprocessed bran
1	T	baking powder
½	tsp	baking soda
¼	C	apple juice concentrate, unsweetened
¼	C	pineapple juice concentrate
2	tsp	honey
¾	C	low-fat buttermilk
2	tsp	vegetable oil
2	tsp	vanilla
4	lg	egg whites, beaten until stiff

1. Pre-heat oven to 350°F. Spray a non-stick 9x5x3 inch loaf pan lightly with a non-stick spray.

2. Combine whole wheat flour, bran, baking powder, and baking soda in a large mixing bowl. Stir to blend.

3. In a separate bowl combine the juice concentrates, honey, buttermilk, oil, and vanilla. Stir to blend.

4. Add dry ingredients to liquid ingredients. Stir quickly until flour disappears. Do not over mix.

5. Mix in beaten egg whites. Fold gently into batter. Immediately fill loaf pan.

6. Bake for 1 hour, or until a toothpick, inserted in center of loaf, comes out dry. Place loaf pan on cake rack for 5 minutes. Remove from pan and complete cooling on cake rack.

Yield: 12 slices

	RCU	FU	Cal	%Fat	P	F	C	Na
Per slice	0	0	133	11	6	2	26	237

Per Slice = 1 Bread exchange

L'Orange and Sherry Sauce

I enjoy preparing this dish on a hot-plate in front of my dinner guests. It gives it that special touch.

2	med	oranges, peeled and quartered, seeds removed (if necessary)
½	C	cooking sherry--OR--
⅓	C	Mountain Cherry juice concentrate
3	T	apple-raspberry juice concentrate, unsweetened
1	tsp	cherry flavor extract
2	tsp	Gifford's Dessert Spice

Spice Substitute:

Instead of Gifford's Dessert Spice, substitute:

1	tsp	banana flavor extract
1	tsp	dried orange peel
1	tsp	Butter Bud Sprinkles
1	tsp	ground cinnamon

Add the banana extract with the juice concentrate, sherry, and cherry extract. Mix together the orange peel, Butter Bud Sprinkles, and cinnamon. Sprinkle evenly over orange quarters as called for in the procedure.

1.   In a skillet combine orange quarters, concentrates, or sherry, and cherry extract. Cook over a low heat until orange quarters are tender (about 5 minutes), turning occasionally.

2.   Spoon orange quarters evenly into 4 dessert dishes. Spoon sauce over top. Top off with Dessert Spice. Serve.

Yield: 4 servings

	RCU	FU	Cal	%Fat	P	F	C	Na
Per Serving	0	0	99	2	1	T	24	10

Per Serving = 1½ Fruit exchange

Menu Shopping List

De-Lites Gourmet Chicken Menu

Poultry
1   lb   chicken breast tenders

Produce
1   sm   yellow onion
               Asparagus, fresh or frozen, desired amount
2   med   oranges

Dairy
1   pint   1% fat cottage cheese, reduced salt
1   qt   low-fat buttermilk
1   doz   eggs (4 eggs required)

Frozen
1   12oz can pineapple juice concentrate
1   12oz can apple-raspberry juice concentrate
1   12oz can Mountain Cherry juice concentrate
1   12oz can apple juice concentrate

Flours / Powders / Starches
1   box   cornstarch
1   bag   whole wheat flour
1   sm   box unprocessed bran
1   sm   container baking powder
1   box   baking soda

Miscellaneous Groceries
1   sm   can low-fat evaporated milk
1   sm   bag long grain brown rice
1   bottle Butter Bud Sprinkles
1   jar   dijon mustard
1   sm   bottle honey
1   bottle vanilla

1	bottle	cherry flavor extract
1	sm	bottle vegetable oil
1	bottle	cooking sherry (optional)

Spices and Seasonings

1	sm	jar beef bouillon granules, low sodium
1	sm	jar chicken bouillon granules, low sodium
1	bottle	Gifford's Gourmet Spice
1	bottle	Gifford's Mexican Spice
1	bottle	Gifford's Dessert Spice
1	bottle	salt
1	bottle	paprika
1	bottle	white pepper

Instead of Gifford's Spices:

1	bottle	onion powder
1	bottle	garlic powder
1	bottle	dill weed
1	bottle	crushed tarragon leaves
1	bottle	ground fennel
1	bottle	ground cardamon
1	bottle	chili powder
1	bottle	red cayenne pepper
1	bottle	orange peel
1	bottle	ground cinnamon
1	bottle	banana flavor extract

To order Gifford's Spices see form in the back of this book.

Remember to check for products you already have on hand.

Holiday

MENU

De-Licious Roast Chicken with Chicken Gravy
Brown Rice and Mushroom Stuffing
Fresh Vegetables and Gourmet Dip
Zucchini and Mushroom Salad Served with
Sweet Pineapple Dressing
Steamed Garden Peas, Pearl Onions, and
Pimentos
Hot Double-Crust Apricot Pie

Roast Chicken with Chicken Gravy

Individual servings of the 10 recipes in this menu total only 1119 Calories with only 8 Percent fat. All of those calories are of healthy origin, not fat. It is possible to serve a feast without guilt, so just enjoy.

4	med	chicken breasts, skin removed
4	med	chicken thighs, skin removed
4	med	chicken legs, skin removed
2	C	water
2	T	Butter Bud Sprinkles
1	T	Gifford's Basic Spice
½	tsp	chicken bouillon granules, low sodium

1.   Pre-heat oven to 375°F.

2.   Arrange chicken pieces evenly in a large baking dish.

3.   Add water, Butter Buds, Basic Spice, and chicken granules. Stir to blend. Cover loosely with foil.

4.   Bake covered 35 minutes. Remove foil and bake uncovered an additional 10 minutes.

Spice Substitute:

Instead of Gifford's Basic Spice, substitute:

2	tsp	chicken bouillon granules, low sodium
2	tsp	onion powder
¼	tsp	ground thyme
⅛	tsp	white pepper

Yield: 4 servings

Gravy

		juice from chicken
2	T	cornstarch, mixed with ⅓ cup cold water
½	C	low-fat evaporated milk

5. Drain chicken juice from baking dish to a saucepan. Bring to a boil.

6. Slowly add cornstarch mixture stirring constantly until sauce thickens. Reduce heat.

7. Add milk. Stir to blend and simmer 5 minutes.

8. Move chicken from baking dish to a serving platter. Pour gravy from the saucepan to a serving dish. Serve.

Yield: approx. 2 Cups, ¼ cup Per Serving

	RCU	FU	Cal	%Fat	P	F	C	Na
Per Serving	0	1	219	20	34	5	8	161

Per Serving = 3 Meat exchange

Brown Rice and Mushroom Stuffing

1	slice	whole wheat bread, toasted and crumbed
1	lg	egg white, cooked and chopped
½	sm	yellow onion, diced
6	med	mushrooms, sliced
1	T	fresh chopped parsley
1	clove	garlic, minced
1	T	Gifford's Basic Spice
2	C	cooked quick brown rice

1.   Combine all ingredients in a 9x13x2 inch baking dish that has been sprayed lightly with a non-stick spray. Stir to blend.

2.   Bake in oven at 375°F for 20 minutes. Serve.

Spice Substitute:

Instead of Gifford's Basic Spice, substitute:

1½	tsp	chicken bouillon granules, low sodium
1½	tsp	onion powder
1	tsp	garlic powder
¼	tsp	paprika
⅛	tsp	white pepper

Yield: 4 servings

	RCU	FU	Cal	%Fat	P	F	C	Na
Per Serving	0	0	138	6	4	1	29	45

Per Serving = ½ Vegetable exchange; 1½ Bread exchange

Fresh Vegetables and Gourmet Dip

Assorted fresh vegetables (your choice)

> carrots sticks
> celery sticks
> broccoli cuts
> cauliflower cuts
> julienne bell peppers and sweet red peppers
> radishes
> cherry tomatoes
> zucchini sticks
> cucumber wedges

1. Rinse vegetables thoroughly before preparing. Arrange vegetables decoratively on a large serving tray. Be creative and festive.

Gourmet Dip

1	C	1% fat cottage cheese, reduce salt
¼	C	apple juice concentrate, unsweetened
¼	C	pineapple juice concentrate
1	T	red wine vinegar
1	T	Butter Bud Sprinkles
¼	tsp	Gifford's Basic Spice
¼	tsp	Gifford's Dessert Spice
¼	tsp	Gifford's Gourmet Spice
¼	tsp	Gifford's Mexican Spice
¼	tsp	Gifford's Italian Spice
¼	tsp	Gifford's Chinese Spice

Spice Substitute:

Instead of Gifford's Spices, substitute:

¼	tsp	chicken bouillon granules, low sodium
¼	tsp	beef bouillon granules, low sodium
¼	tsp	onion powder
¼	tsp	garlic powder
¼	tsp	thyme

¼	tsp	paprika
¼	tsp	ground cloves
¼	tsp	ground cinnamon
⅛	tsp	chili powder
⅛	tsp	curry powder
⅛	tsp	ground ginger
⅛	tsp	white pepper

2.   Combine all ingredients in a blender. Mix until smooth.

3.   Chill if desired. Serve with fresh vegetables.

Yield: approx. 2 cups

	RCU	FU	Cal	%Fat	P	F	C	Na
Per ½ Cup	0	0	104	6	7	T	17	23

Per ½ Cup = 1 Fruit exchange

Zucchini and Mushroom Salad

2	med	zucchini, 1 sliced thin, 1 grated
8	med	mushrooms, sliced
4	C	shredded lettuce
2	tsp	Gifford's Basic Spice
1	tsp	Gifford's Gourmet Spice
8	leaves	red leaf lettuce

Spice Substitute:

Instead of Gifford's Basic and Gourmet Spice, substitute:

1	tsp	chicken bouillon granules, low sodium
1	tsp	onion powder
½	tsp	thyme
½	tsp	paprika
½	tsp	garlic powder
⅛	tsp	crushed tarragon leaves
⅛	tsp	ground clove

1. In a large salad bowl combine the sliced zucchini, mushrooms, and shredded lettuce. Add spices and toss gently to blend.

2. Arrange 2 red leaf lettuce leaves onto each of 4 salad plates. Place zucchini and mushroom salad evenly over red leaves. Top with grated zucchini. Serve.

Yield: 4 salads

	RCU	FU	Cal	%Fat	P	F	C	Na
Per Serving	0	0	33	12	2	T	6	10

Per Serving = 1 Vegetable exchange

Sweet Pineapple Dressing

1	C	1% fat cottage cheese, reduced salt
1	C	crushed pineapple , unsweetened
2	T	Orchard Peach juice concentrate
1	tsp	Butter Bud Sprinkles
1	tsp	Gifford's Dessert Spice

Spice Substitute:

Instead of Gifford's Dessert Spice, substitute:

½	tsp	ground cinnamon
½	tsp	ground cloves

1. Combine all ingredients in a blender. Mix until smooth. Chill before serving if desired.

Yield: 2 cups

	RCU	FU	Cal	%Fat	P	F	C	Na
Per ½ Cup	0	0	95	7	7	T	16	233

Per ½ Cup = 1 Fruit exchange

Steamed Garden Peas, Pearl Onions, and Pimentos

1	16oz	bag frozen peas
1	16oz	bag pearl onions
2	T	diced pimentos
½	C	water

1. Combine ingredients in a saucepan. Bring to a boil. Reduce heat and cover. Simmer 5 to 7 minutes. Drain then serve.

Yield: 4 servings

	RCU	FU	Cal	%Fat	P	F	C	Na
Per Serving	0	0	108	5	7	T	20	271

Per Serving = ½ Vegetable exchange; 1 Bread exchange

Hot Double-Crust Apricot Pie Filling

2	12oz	bags dried apricots
1	C	Orchard Peach juice concentrate
1	C	water
¼	C	apple juice concentrate, unsweetened
2	T	Butter Bud Sprinkles
2	tsp	Gifford's Dessert Spice
1	T	cornstarch, mixed with 3 T cold water

Spice Substitute:

Instead of Gifford's Dessert Spice, substitute:

| 1 | tsp | ground cinnamon |
| ½ | tsp | ground cloves |

1. Combine the apricots, Orchard Peach juice concentrate, water, apple juice concentrate, Butter Buds, and Dessert Spice in a saucepan. Stir to blend.

2. Bring to a boil. Reduce heat and simmer 15 minutes.

3.	Slowly add cornstarch mixture stirring constantly until mixture thickens. Remove from heat.

Double Crust Pie Dough

¾	C	oat bran
½	C	oat bran graham crackers, finely crumbed
2	T	Butter Bud Sprinkles
1	tsp	baking powder
¼	tsp	salt
2	lg	egg whites, slightly beaten
1	T	vegetable oil
¼	C	Orchard Peach juice concentrate
1	T	honey
1	C	whole wheat flour (use when kneading dough mixture)

4.	Stir together the oat bran, crumbed graham crackers, Butter Buds, baking powder, and salt.

5.	In a separate bowl combine the egg whites, oil, Orchard Peach concentrate, and honey. Stir to blend.

6.	Add liquid mixture slowly to flour mixture, stirring with a fork or a slotted spoon until just combined.

7.	Divide the dough into 2 parts and form into 2 balls with a fork.

To make bottom crust:

8.	Place 1 dough ball on a well floured surface (using a pastry cloth will help prevent sticking). Flatten dough and smooth edges with your hands.

9.	Roll from center to edge; adding wheat flour in small amounts, forming a circle about 12 inches in diameter.

10.	Wrap pastry around rolling pin for easy transfer to pie plate. To do so, lift pastry cloth with pastry on it as pastry rolls around pin.

11.	Gently unroll pastry onto a 9 inch pie plate. To repair tears, gently press back together. Ease pastry into pie plate.

12. Trim the edge of the pastry 1 inch beyond the edge of the pie plate. Fold under the extra pastry to reinforce the edge. Flute edge of pastry (press dough with forefinger outside the pie plate) while using the thumb and forefinger of other hand inside of pie plate.

For top crust:

12. Roll out second ball of dough. Cut slits in center to allow steam to escape while baking.

13. Place the apricot filling in the pie shell.

14. Wrap the pastry around the rolling pin and unroll onto the filled pie. Trim the edge ½ inch beyond the edge. Fold extra pastry under the edge of bottom crust. Flute edge.

15. Bake in a pre-heated oven at 350°F for 20 to 25 minutes, or until crust is golden brown.

Yield: 8 servings

	RCU	FU	Cal	%Fat	P	F	C	Na
Per Serving	0	½	422	8	8	4	98	230

Per Serving = 8 Fruit exchange; 1 Bread exchange; ½ Fat exchange

Menu Shopping List

De-licious Roast Chicken with Chicken Gravy Menu

Poultry
4	med	packages chicken breast
4	med	chicken thighs
4	med	chicken legs

Produce
		assorted fresh vegetables for dipping, your choice
1	sm	yellow onion
10	med	mushrooms
1	sm	bunch fresh parsley
1	sm	bud garlic
2	med	zucchini squash
1	sm	head iceberg lettuce
1	med	head red leaf lettuce

Dairy
| 1 | doz | eggs (2 eggs required) |
| 1 | pint | 1% fat cottage cheese, reduced salt |

Frozen
1	12oz	can pineapple juice concentrate
1	12oz	can Orchard Peach juice concentrate
1	12oz	can apple juice concentrate
1	16oz	bag frozen peas
1	16oz	bag frozen pearl onions

Flours / Powders / Starches
1	bottle	Butter Bud Sprinkles
1	can	low-fat evaporated milk
1	box	quick brown rice
1	loaf	whole wheat bread

1	bottle	red wine vinegar
1	15oz	can crushed pineapple
1	sm	jar diced pimentos
2	12oz	bags dried apricot
1	box	oat bran graham crackers
1	sm	bottle honey
1	sm	bottle vegetable oil

Spices and Seasonings

1	sm	jar chicken bouillon granules, low sodium
		salt
1	bottle	Gifford's Basic Spice
1	bottle	Gifford's Dessert Spice
1	bottle	Gifford's Gourmet Spice
1	bottle	Gifford's Mexican Spice
1	bottle	Gifford's Italian Spice
1	bottle	Gifford's Chinese Spice

To order Gifford's Spices see form in the back of this book.

Instead of Gifford's Spices:

1	bottle	onion powder
1	bottle	thyme
1	bottle	white pepper
1	bottle	garlic powder
1	bottle	paprika
1	bottle	ground clove
1	bottle	ground cinnamon
1	bottle	chili powder
1	bottle	curry powder
1	bottle	ground ginger
1	bottle	crushed tarragon leaves

Remember to check products on hand.

MENU

De-Licious Eggs Benedict
Golden Hashbrown Potatoes
A Special Orange Juice
Chilled Fresh Fruit (your choice)
De-Lites Hot Bran Muffins and
Sweet Berry Preserves

De-Licious Eggs Benedict

2		whole wheat english muffins
4	1oz	slices turkey-ham
4		eggs

1. Toast english muffins.

2. In a skillet sprayed lightly with a non-stick spray, lightly brown the turkey-ham slices over a medium-low heat.

3. In a saucepan bring 1 quart water to a boil. Add ½ teaspoon salt. Reduce heat to medium. Crack eggs into water.

4. Poach eggs for approximately 4 minutes, or until egg whites are cooked through. Remove eggs using a slotted spoon.

5. Place 1 muffin half onto each of 4 serving plates. Layer one slice of the turkey-ham, and one egg over each muffin half.

   Yield: 4 servings

De-lites Hollandaise Sauce

1	C	De-lites cream cheese(see recipe on page 14)
1	tsp	lemon juice
1	tsp	onion powder
½	tsp	chicken bouillon granules, low sodium
1	tsp	prepared mustard

1.   In a small mixing bowl combine ingredients. Stir gently to blend.

2.   Let sauce stand at room temperature a few minutes, or microwave on a low setting to serve warm.

3.   Spoon hollandaise sauce evenly over eggs benedict. Serve.

Yields: 1¼ cups

	RCU	FU	Cal	%Fat	P	F	C	Na
Per Serving	0	1	248	31	21	8	20	583

Per Serving = 1 Bread exchange; 2 Meat exchange; ½ Fat exchange

Golden Hashbrown Potatoes

| 2 | med | potatoes, scrubbed and rinsed thoroughly |
| 2 | tsp | Gifford's Basic Spice |

Spice Substitute:

Instead of Gifford's Basic Spice, substitute:

½	tsp	onion powder
½	tsp	garlic powder
½	tsp	thyme
½	tsp	black pepper

1.   Cook potatoes covered in boiling water until tender, 30 to 40 minutes. Remove from water. Cool.

2.   Grate potatoes into a mixing bowl. Using your hands, form 4 potato squares.

3.　　　Place potato squares in a large skillet sprayed lightly with a non-stick spray. Cook over medium heat until golden brown on both sides.

4.　　　Sprinkle Basic Spice evenly over the top. Serve.

Yield: 4 servings

	RCU	FU	Cal	%Fat	P	F	C	Na
Per Hashbrown	0	0	48	2	1	T	11	4

Per Hashbrown Square = ½ Bread exchange

A Special Orange Juice

1	lg	ripe banana
1	lg	orange, peeled and quartered
½	C	Orange-Banana-Pineapple juice concentrate
1	tsp	lime juice
½	C	water
½	C	skim milk
2	tsp	dried orange peel
1	tsp	Gifford's Dessert Spice

Spice Substitute:

Instead of Gifford's Dessert Spice, substitute:

¼	tsp	ground cinnamon
¼	tsp	ground nutmeg

1.　　　Combine all ingredients in a blender. Puree 30 seconds, then blend on high speed until smooth and fluffy. Serve at once.

Yield: 4 (6 oz) servings

	RCU	FU	Cal	%Fat	P	F	C	Na
Per 6 Oz.	0	0	142	3	3	T	34	18

Per 6 Oz. = 2 Fruit exchange

De-Lites Hot Bran Muffins

1½	C	unprocessed bran
1	C	whole wheat flour
1½	tsp	baking powder
½	tsp	baking soda
¼	tsp	salt
3	lg	egg whites, slightly beaten
¼	C	apple juice concentrate, unsweetened
¼	C	Orchard Peach juice concentrate
2	tsp	vegetable oil
1½	C	skim milk

1. In a large mixing bowl combine unprocessed bran, whole wheat flour, baking powder, baking soda, and salt. Stir well to blend.

2. Make a well in center of flour mixture. Add remaining ingredients to well. Stir to blend.

3. Spray a teflon muffin pan lightly with a non-stick spray. Spoon muffin mixture into pan, filling each cup ⅔ full.

4. Bake in a 375°F oven 25 minutes, or until golden brown.

    Yield: 12 muffins

	RCU	FU	Cal	%Fat	P	F	C	Na
Per Muffin	0	0	110	15	5	2	20	199

Per Muffin = 1 Bread exchange

Menu Shopping List

De-Licious Eggs Benedict Menu

Poultry
1	sm	roll Turkey-Ham

Produce
2	med	potatoes
1	lg	banana
1	lg	orange

Dairy
1	doz	eggs (4 eggs required)
1	pint	skim milk
1	pint	1% fat cottage cheese, reduced salt

Frozen
1	12oz	can Orange-Banana-Pineapple juice concentrate
1	12oz	can Mountain Cherry juice concentrate
1	12oz	can apple juice concentrate
1	16oz	bag frozen Boysenberries
1	12oz	can Orchard Peach juice concentrate

Flours / Powders / Starches
1		bag of 6 whole wheat english muffins
1	box	unprocessed bran
1	sm	bag whole wheat flour
1	box	baking soda
1	sm	container baking powder
1	box	cornstarch

Miscellaneous Groceries
1	sm	bottle lemon juice
1	sm	bottle prepared mustard
1	sm	bottle lime juice
1	sm	bottle vegetable oil

| 1 | sm | bottle honey |
| 1 | bottle | cherry flavor extract |

Spices and Seasonings

1	sm	bottle chicken bouillon granules, low sodium
1	sm	bottle onion powder
1	sm	bottle orange peel
	bottle	salt
1	bottle	Gifford's Basic Spice
1	bottle	Gifford's Dessert Spice

To order Gifford's Spices see form in the back of this book.

Instead of Gifford's Spices:

1	bottle	garlic powder
1	bottle	thyme
1	bottle	black pepper
1	bottle	ground cinnamon
1	bottle	ground nutmeg

MENU

Spicy Turkey-Ham and Skillet Potatoes with Homemade Tortillas
Smoked Cheeseball and Crackers
A Special Eggnog
Holiday Fruit Gelatin Salad
Yeast Free Banana Raisin Bread with Golden Banana Topping

Spicy Turkey-Ham with Skillet Potatoes

My television viewers usually let me know what their favorites are. This recipe is one of them. I hope it will become one of yours.

1	lb	turkey-ham, rinse under cold water and cut into 1-inch cubes
1	sm	onion, cut julienne
1	sm	bell pepper, cut julienne
1	sm	sweet red pepper, cut julienne
2	cloves	garlic, minced
8	med	mushrooms, sliced
1	4oz	can diced green chilies
¼	C	apple juice concentrate, unsweetened
2	T	worcestershire sauce
2	15oz	can whole tomatoes, no salt added
2	med	potatoes, sliced thin
1	C	frozen peas
1	C	frozen crinkle cut carrots
2	T	Gifford's Mexican Spice
2	T	fresh chopped parsley

Spice Substitute:

Instead of Gifford's Mexican Spice, substitute:

1	T	onion powder
1	T	garlic powder
1½	tsp	beef bouillon granules, low sodium
1½	tsp	chicken bouillon granules, low sodium
1	tsp	chili powder
1	tsp	ground cumin
1	tsp	ground oregano
½	tsp	ground cloves

1. Lightly spray a large saucepan with a non-stick spray. In saucepan saute the turkey-ham, onion, bell pepper, red pepper, and garlic over a medium-high heat until vegetables are tender.

2. Add the mushrooms, diced chilies, apple juice concentrate, and worcestershire sauce. Stir.

3. Add the tomatoes, potatoes, peas, carrots, Mexican Spice, and parsley. Stir gently to blend. Reduce heat. Cover.

4. Simmer mixture approximately 15 minutes, or until potatoes are tender. Stir occasionally. Serve.
   Yield: 6 servings

	RCU	FU	Cal	%Fat	P	F	C	Na
Per Serving	0	1	248	18	20	5	33	696

Per Serving = 2 Vegetable exchange; 1 Bread exchange; 2 Meat exchange

Homemade Tortillas

On page 10 or substitute commercial whole wheat tortillas

Smoked Cheeseball with Crackers

Once in a while, when up in front of an audience, things don't go quite as planned. One evening I was using an electric hand mixer. The mixer had a mind of its own. Ingredients were flying all over and I couldn't turn it off. Needless to say, the class had many more surprises. Entertainment at its finest - the "I Love Lucy" way.

1	C	1% fat cottage cheese, reduced salt
1	C	low-fat Ricotta cheese
3	T	Grape Nuts crumbed
1	tsp	Gifford's Basic Spice
½	tsp	Gifford's Italian Spice
2	T	Orchard Peach juice concentrate
1	drop	liquid smoke
1	C	Grape Nuts, finely crumbed (set aside)
		crackers of your choice

Spice Substitute:

Instead of Gifford's Basic and Italian Spice, substitute:

1	tsp	chicken bouillon granules, low sodium
1	tsp	onion powder
1	tsp	garlic powder
¼	tsp	thyme
¼	tsp	white pepper

1. In a bowl combine all ingredients, except the 1 cup Grape Nuts. Mix until well blended. Form mixture into a large ball.

2. Pour the crushed Grape Nuts onto a plate, or shallow dish. Spread out evenly. Roll cheeseball evenly over Grape Nuts until coated.

3. Place cheeseball in center of serving dish. Place crackers of your choice around cheeseball.

When serving: Dip cracker into cheese ball or use a dinner knife to spread desired amount onto crackers.

Note: When shopping for crackers be sure to read the label in order to choose those with the best nutritional value.

Yield: 6 servings

	RCU	FU	Cal	%Fat	P	F	C	Na
Per Serving	0	1	186	19	12	4	25	278

Per Serving = 1 Bread exchange; 1 Meat exchange

A Special Eggnog

1	small	ripe banana, optional
2	C	low-fat evaporated milk
¼	C	apple juice concentrate, unsweetened
¼	C	Orchard Peach juice concentrate
1	T	honey
1	tsp	vanilla
1	T	Butter Bud Sprinkles
2	tsp	Gifford's Dessert Spice
½	C	crushed ice

Spice Substitute:

Instead of Gifford's Dessert Spice, substitute:

1	tsp	banana flavor extract
½	tsp	cinnamon
¼	tsp	ground allspice
¼	tsp	ground anise seed
¼	tsp	ground cloves
¼	tsp	ground nutmeg

1. Combine in a blender all ingredients. Mix on whip speed until well blended. Serve immediately.
    Yield: 4 servings

	RCU	FU	Cal	%Fat	P	F	C	Na
Per Serving	0	0	212	3	10	T	42	159

Per Serving = 1 Milk exchange; 1½ Fruit exchange

Holiday Fruit Gelatin Salad

½	C	water
1	env	unflavored gelatin
⅔	C	Mountain Cherry juice concentrate
⅓	C	water
1	tsp	cherry flavor extract

1	16oz	bag Fruit Medley
1	C	De-Lites Cream Cheese (see recipe on page 14)
1	T	Gifford's Dessert Spice

Spice Substitute:

Instead of Gifford's Dessert Spice, substitute:

1	T	crumbed Grape Nuts
½	tsp	ground cinnamon
¼	tsp	ground allspice
½	tsp	dried orange peel

1. In a small bowl pour the ½ cup water. Sprinkle the unflavored gelatine over the top. Let stand 1 minute.

2. In a saucepan combine the Mountain Cherry juice concentrate, ⅓ cup water, and cherry extract. Bring to a boil.

3. Stir into gelatin mixture until completely dissolved. Pour into 8½ X 8½ pan. Chill until partially set.

4. Add Fruit Medley to gelatin evenly, pushing gently to blend. Chill until set.

5. When serving: cut gelatin mixture evenly into 6 squares. Spoon onto serving plates. Top off with a dollop of cream cheese. Sprinkle Dessert Spice over top.

Yield: 6 servings.

	RCU	FU	Cal	%Fat	P	F	C	Na
Per Serving	0	0	176	3	7	T	35	107

Per Serving = 2 Fruit exchange

Yeast Free Banana Raisin Bread

2¼	C	whole wheat flour
½	C	unprocessed bran
1	tsp	baking powder

¼	tsp	baking soda
3	med	ripe bananas, mashed and well blended
¼	C	apple juice concentrate, unsweetened
⅔	C	buttermilk
2	tsp	honey
2	tsp	vanilla
2	tsp	vegetable oil
½	C	raisins, plumped in ¼ cup hot fresh orange juice for 15 minutes
1	tsp	almond extract, added to raisins and juice
4	lg	egg whites, beaten until stiff

1.   Pre-heat oven to 375°F. Spray a non-stick 9x5x3 inch loaf pan lightly with non-stick spray.

2.   Combine whole wheat flour, bran, baking powder, and baking soda in a mixing bowl.

3.   In a separate bowl combine mashed bananas, apple juice concentrate, buttermilk, honey, vanilla, oil, and raisins with orange juice and almond extract.

4.   Add dry ingredients to wet ingredients and stir quickly until flour disappears. Do not over mix. Mix in beaten egg whites.

5.   Immediately fill loaf pan with mixture and place in oven. Lower temperature to 350°F and bake for 1 hour, or until golden brown.

Note: Test for readiness by inserting a toothpick. When it comes out clean, bread is finished baking. Bread will shrink slightly from sides of pan when done.

6.   Place loaf pan on cake rack for 5 minutes. Remove bread from pan and complete cooling on rack.

Yield: 12 slices

	RCU	FU	Cal	%Fat	P	F	C	Na
Per Slice	0	0	156	9	6	2	32	108

Per Slice = 1 Fruit exchange; 1 Bread exchange

Golden Banana Topping

2	med	bananas, sliced
1/3	C	pineapple juice concentrate
1/2	C	water
2	tsp	imitation banana extract
1	T	Butter Bud Sprinkles
1	tsp	Gifford's Dessert Spice
1	T	cornstarch, mixed with 3 T cold water

Spice Substitute:

Instead of Gifford's Dessert Spice, substitute:

1/2	tsp	ground cinnamon
1/4	tsp	ground allspice

1. Spray a skillet lightly with non-stick spray.

2. Place 1/2 of the bananas into skillet. Cook bananas over medium heat until browned (about 2 minutes). Remove banana slices from skillet to a platter and set aside.

3. Add pineapple juice concentrate, water, banana extract, Butter Bud Sprinkles, and Dessert Spice to skillet. Stir to blend. Bring mixture to a boil. Reduce heat.

4. Slowly add cornstarch mixture stirring constantly until thick.

5. Add remaining bananas. Stir. Simmer sauce until bananas break up and blend into sauce. Remove from heat.

6. Add browned banana slices. Stir. Serve over Banana Raisin Bread slices.

    Yield: approx. 2 cups

	RCU	FU	Cal	%Fat	P	F	C	Na
Per 1/2 Cup	0	0	107	3	1	T	26	1

Per 1/2 Cup = 1 1/2 Fruit exchange

Menu Shopping List

Spicy Turkey-Ham and Skillet Potatoes Menu

Poultry
1	sm	turkey-ham, lower salt

Produce
1	sm	yellow onion
1	sm	bell pepper
1		sweet red pepper
1	bud	garlic
8	med	mushrooms
2	med	potatoes
1	sm	bunch parsley
6	med	bananas

Dairy
1	doz	eggs (4 eggs required)
1	qt	container 1% cottage cheese, reduced salt
1	sm	container low-fat Ricotta Cheese
1	qt	low-fat Buttermilk

Frozen
1	12oz	can apple juice concentrate
1	12oz	can Orchard Peach juice concentrate
1	12oz	can Mountain Cherry juice concentrate
1	12oz	can pineapple juice concentrate
1	16oz	bag Fruit Medley
1	16oz	bag crinkle cut carrots
1	16oz	bag frozen peas
1	12oz	can orange juice concentrate

Flours / Powders / Starches
1	sm	bag whole wheat flour
1	sm	bag whole wheat pastry flour --or--
1	sm	bag Gold Medal Oat Blend flour

1	sm	box oat bran
1	sm	box unprocessed bran
1	box	cornstarch
1	sm	container baking powder
1	box	baking soda
1	sm	box Grape Nuts cereal

Miscellaneous Groceries

1	4oz	can diced green chilies
4	15oz	cans whole tomatoes, no salt added
2	cans	low-fat evaporated milk
1	bottle	honey
1	box	unflavored gelatin
1	bottle	vanilla
1	sm	bottle vegetable oil
1	box	raisins
1	bottle	Butter Bud Sprinkles
1	bottle	cherry flavor extract
1	bottle	liquid smoke
1	bottle	almond extract
1	bottle	worcestershire sauce

Spices and Seasonings

		salt
1	bottle	Gifford's Mexican Spice
1	bottle	Gifford's Basic Spice
1	bottle	Gifford's Dessert Spice
1	bottle	Gifford's Italian Spice

To order Gifford's Spices see form in the back of this book.

If not using Gifford's Spices review recipes for alternate spices required.

Remember to check products you have on hand.

MENU

Traditional Turkey Dinner with all the Trimmings

Roasted Turkey with
Onion Bread Stuffing(Dressing)
De-Licious Turkey Gravy
A Special Holiday Yam
Old Fashioned Mashed Potatoes
Fresh Cranberry Sauce
Chilled Garden Salad with
De-Lites Basic Dressing
Steamed Carrots and Peas
Fruit Cocktail Salad
De-Lites Whole Wheat Bread
Fresh Hot Mincemeat Pie
Fresh Pumpkin Pie

With a total of 15 recipes, this is my all-time favorite menu to instruct. In dozens of classes I have completely prepared everything in two hours. Scores of families have prepared this menu for Thanksgiving and loved it! Rewards in a profession come in many ways, and just having the opportunity to hear the enthusiastic response from my new friends is, simply put, priceless.

Roasted Turkey and De-Licious Turkey Gravy

1		10-12lb young turkey, skin and wings removed and discarded
2	C	water
1	T	Butter Bud Sprinkles
2	tsp	chicken bouillon granules, low sodium
2	tsp	onion powder
2	tsp	Gifford's Basic Spice
3	T	cornstarch
1	C	low-fat evaporated milk

Spice Substitute:

Instead of Gifford's Basic Spice, substitute:

1	tsp	chicken bouillon granules, low sodium, additional
1	tsp	onion powder, additional
1	tsp	garlic powder
¼	tsp	white pepper

1. Pre-heat oven to 375°F.

2. Stuff bird loosely with dressing. Place turkey in a large, deep roasting pan.

3. Add the water, Butter Buds, chicken granules, and spices to the pan. Stir to blend.

4. Cover with roasting pan lid, or cover completely with foil, but do not allow foil to touch bird. Roast bird approximately 2 hours, allowing additional time for larger birds.

5. Remove cover at the 1½ hour mark of roasting time, to allow browning. Baste once or twice with juice.

6. Remove bird to a serving platter. Keep warm. Remove stuffing from cavity. Keep warm.

7. Drain juice to a saucepan. Bring to a boil.

8. Add 3 tablespoons cornstarch mixed with ½ cup cold water. Stirring constantly until thick. Reduce heat.

9.   Add 1 cup low-fat evaporated milk. Stir to blend. Simmer 5 minutes.

10.   Carve turkey as desired. Turkey, stuffing and gravy are ready to
        serve.

        Yields: 6 servings

	RCU	FU	Cal	%Fat	P	F	C	Na
Per Serving	0	1	284	18	45	6	10	185

Per Serving = 4 Meat exchange

Onion Bread Stuffing (Dressing)

8	slices	dry whole wheat bread
1	med	onion, diced
1	C	water
1	T	Butter Bud Sprinkles
1	T	onion powder
2	tsp	Gifford's Basic Spice
1	tsp	chicken bouillon granules, low sodium

Spice Substitute:

Instead of Gifford's Basic Spice, substitute:

1	tsp	chicken bouillon granules, low sodium, additional
½	tsp	thyme
¼	tsp	white pepper

1.   In a large bowl break bread slices into small pieces.

2.   Add diced onion. Stir to blend.

3.   In a saucepan bring to a boil the water, Butter Buds, onion powder,
        Basic Spice, and chicken granules. Stir.

4.   Pour broth slowly over bread and onions stirring to blend.

5.   Stuff loosely into the bird cavity.

For Sage Dressing add these ingredients:

2	stalks	celery, diced
2	tsp	sage
½	tsp	ground caraway seed(optional)

6. Add celery to bread and onions in bowl. Add spices to broth in saucepan.

Yield: 6 servings

	RCU	FU	Cal	%Fat	P	F	C	Na
Per Serving	0	0	94	10	4	1	19	183

Per Serving = ½ Vegetable exchange; 1 Bread exchange

A Special Holiday Yam

| 1 | lg | yam, peeled, cut into 1½ inch pieces |

Blend together the following:

1	15oz	can small red beans, unsweetened
½	C	Orchard Peach juice concentrate
½	C	apple juice concentrate, unsweetened
2	T	Butter Bud Sprinkles
1	T	Gifford's Dessert Spice
3	T	honey
½	C	raisins
½	C	De-Lites Cream Cheese, slightly whipped (see recipe on page 14).

Spice Substitute:

Instead of Gifford's Dessert Spice, substitute:

| 1 | tsp | ground cinnamon |
| ½ | tsp | ground cloves |

| ¼ | tsp | ground allspice |
| ¼ | tsp | ground anise seed |

1. Place yams in a medium-size saucepan. Pour sauce, from the blender, over yams. Stir and cover.

2. Cook over medium heat, stirring frequently for 25 minutes.

3. When serving, spoon cream cheese around and between yams for a swirl look.

Yield: 4 servings

	RCU	FU	Cal	%Fat	P	F	C	Na
Per Serving	0	0	369	3	12	1	82	85

Per Serving = 4 Fruit exchange; 2 Bread exchange

Old Fashioned Mashed Potatoes

2	lg	potatoes, peeled, cut into small pieces
2	C	water
1½	T	Butter Bud Sprinkles
2	tsp	onion powder
1½	tsp	chicken bouillon granules, low sodium
⅛	tsp	white pepper
½	C	low-fat evaporated milk

1. In a saucepan bring to a boil the potatoes and water. Reduce heat. Cover.

2. Simmer potatoes 12 minutes, or until tender. Remove cover.

3. Add remaining ingredients. Reduce heat to low.

4. Mash potato mixture, right in the pan, using a whisk or potato masher. Remove from heat. Cover until ready to serve.

Yield: 4 servings

	RCU	FU	Cal	%Fat	P	F	C	Na
Per Serving	0	0	96	2	4	T	20	43

Per Serving = 1 Bread exchange

Fresh Cranberry Sauce

1	C	apple-raspberry juice concentrate, unsweetened
1	C	whole fresh cranberries
1	T	Butter Bud Sprinkles
1	tsp	Gifford's Dessert Spice

Spice Substitute:

Instead of Gifford's Dessert Spice, substitute:

½	tsp	ground cinnamon
½	tsp	ground allspice
⅛	tsp	ground cloves

1. Combine all ingredients in a saucepan. Bring to a boil. Reduce heat and cover.

2. Simmer 8 to 10 minutes then remove from heat. Stir well using a whisk. Serve hot or cold.

    Yield: approx. 2 cups

	RCU	FU	Cal	%Fat	P	F	C	Na
Per ¼ Cup	0	0	66	2	T	T	16	9

Per ¼ Cup = 1 Fruit exchange

Chilled Garden Salad

1	sm	head iceberg lettuce, rinsed, drained, and torn into small pieces
1	sm	carrot, shredded
1	sm	cucumber, thinly sliced

| 2 | sm | tomatoes, carefully cut into small pieces |
| 2 | tsp | Gifford's Basic Spice |

Spice Substitute:

Instead of Gifford's Basic Spice, substitute:

1	tsp	onion powder
1	tsp	garlic powder
1	tsp	ground thyme
½	tsp	black pepper
½	tsp	paprika

1.   Combine all ingredients in a large salad bowl. Gently toss to blend. Cover. Chill a few minutes before serving.

Yield: 4 to 6 servings

	RCU	FU	Cal	%Fat	P	F	C	Na
Per Serving	0	0	34	10	1	T	7	14

Per Serving = 1 Vegetable exchange

De-Lites Basic Dressing

1½	C	1% fat cottage cheese, reduced salt
½	C	water
2	T	dill pickle juice
2	T	pineapple juice concentrate
1	T	diced pimentos
1	T	Butter Bud Sprinkles
2	tsp	Gifford's Basic Spice
1	tsp	chicken bouillon granules, low sodium

Spice Substitute:

Instead of Gifford's Basic Spice, substitute:

| 2 | tsp | beef bouillon granules, low sodium |
| 2 | tsp | onion powder |

1	tsp	garlic powder
1	tsp	paprika
½	tsp	ground thyme
¼	tsp	white pepper

1. Blend all ingredients until smooth and creamy. Chill if desired before serving.

   Yield: approx. 2 cups

	RCU	FU	Cal	%Fat	P	F	C	Na
Per ¼Cup	0	0	47	11	6	1	5	102

Per ½ Cup = ½ Milk exchange

Steamed Carrots and Peas

1	16oz	bag frozen crinkle cut carrots
1	16oz	bag frozen peas
1	C	water

1. Combine in a saucepan. Cover. Steam 7 minutes or until bright in color and tender.

   Yield: 6 servings

	RCU	FU	Cal	%Fat	P	F	C	Na
Per Serving	0	0	88	5	5	T	17	129

Per Serving = 1 Vegetable exchange; 1 Bread exchange

Fruit Cocktail Salad

2	16oz	cans lite fruit cocktail in pear juice, no sugar added, drained
1	C	De-Lites Cream Cheese (see recipe on page 14)
1	med	banana, sliced
½	C	raisins
2	T	pineapple juice concentrate

| 1 | tsp | Gifford's Dessert Spice |
| 1 | tsp | almond extract |

Spice Substitute:

Instead of Gifford's Dessert Spice, substitute:

1	tsp	banana flavor extract
½	tsp	dried orange peel
½	tsp	ground cinnamon
⅛	tsp	ground allspice

1.   Combine ingredients in a salad bowl. Gently fold ingredients until blended. Chill if desired before serving.

   Yield: 4 to 6 servings

	RCU	FU	Cal	%Fat	P	F	C	Na
Per Serving	0	0	173	3	6	1	38	161

Per Serving = 2 Fruit exchange

De-Lites Whole Wheat Bread

2¼	C	whole wheat flour
½	C	unprocessed bran
1	tsp	baking powder
½	tsp	baking soda
¼	C	pineapple juice concentrate
¼	C	apple juice concentrate, unsweetened
2	tsp	honey
¾	C	buttermilk
2	tsp	vegetable oil
2	tsp	vanilla
4	lg	egg whites, beaten until stiff

1.   Pre-heat oven to 375°F. Spray a 9x5x3 inch loaf pan lightly with a non-stick spray.

2. Combine wheat flour, bran, baking powder, and baking soda in a mixing bowl. In a separate bowl, combine juice concentrates, honey, buttermilk, oil, and vanilla.

3. Add dry ingredients to wet ingredients and stir quickly until flour disappears. Do not over mix. Fold in beaten egg whites.

4. Immediately fill loaf pan and place in oven. Lower temperature to 350°F and bake for 1 hour or until golden brown.

5. Place loaf pan on cake rack for 5 minutes. Remove from pan and complete cooling on a rack.

Yield: approx. 10 slices

	RCU	FU	Cal	%Fat	P	F	C	Na
Per Slice	0	0	267	11	11	3	53	275

Per Slice = ½ Fruit exchange; 2½ Bread exchange

Fresh Pumpkin Pie Filling

4	lg	egg whites, slightly beaten
1	15oz	can pumpkin
2	T	Gifford's Dessert Spice
½	C	low-fat evaporated milk
⅓	C	Orchard Peach juice concentrate
1	T	honey

Spice Substitute:

Instead of Gifford's Dessert Spice, substitute:

2	tsp	ground cinnamon
1	tsp	ground cloves
½	tsp	ground nutmeg
2	tsp	Butter Bud Sprinkles

1.   Combine ingredients in a mixing bowl in the order listed; stir between each addition.

Crust

| 1 | C | oat bran graham crackers, finely crumbled |
| 3 | T | Orchard Peach juice concentrate |

2.   Place graham cracker crumbs in a small bowl. Add Orchard Peach concentrate, a tablespoon at a time, while cutting with a large spoon.

3.   When mixture is crumbly, pour into a pie plate that has been sprayed lightly with a non-stick spray. Spread crumbs evenly, pressing gently until crust is ⅔ to the top of pan on the sides, and smooth.

4.   Pour filling in shell. Cover pie. Bake in oven at 325°F for 1 hour.

5.   Remove cover and bake an additional 10 minutes to brown. Insert a wooden toothpick to center of pie. If toothpick comes out dry, pie is done.

6.   Cool pie on a rack 10 minutes or so before serving. Top off with De-Lites Cream Cheese. If desired, see recipe on page 14.

Yield: 8 servings

	RCU	FU	Cal	%Fat	P	F	C	Na
Per Serving	0	0	120	10	5	1	24	124

Per Serving = ½ Fruit exchange; 1 Bread exchange

Fresh Hot Mincemeat Pie

1	lg	red apple, pared, cored and diced
1	C	currants
½	C	chopped dates, unsweetened
½	C	raisins
⅔	C	apple juice concentrate, unsweetened
1	T	honey

2	T	Butter Bud Sprinkles
1	T	Gifford's Dessert Spice

Spice Substitute:

Instead of Gifford's Dessert Spice, substitute:

1	tsp	ground cinnamon
1	tsp	ground cloves
1	tsp	allspice
½	tsp	anise seed

1. Combine all ingredients in a saucepan. Bring to a boil. Reduce heat. Cover. Simmer 10 to 12 minutes stirring occasionally.

Double Crust Pie Dough

1	C	oat bran
½	C	oat bran graham crackers, finely crumbled
2	T	Butter Bud Sprinkles
1	tsp	baking powder
¼	tsp	salt
2	lg	egg whites, slightly beaten
1	T	vegetable oil
¼	C	Orchard Peach juice concentrate
1	T	honey
1	C	whole wheat flour (used when kneading dough mixture)

2. Stir together the oat bran, crumbled graham crackers, Butter Bud Sprinkles, baking powder, and salt in a bowl.

3. In a separate bowl combine the egg whites, oil, Orchard Peach concentrate, and honey. Stir to blend.

4. Slowly add liquid mixture to flour mixture, stirring with a fork or a slotted spoon until combined.

5. Add small amounts of the whole wheat flour, mixing with your hand to form a ball that is smooth. Divide the dough into two parts and form into two separate balls.

6.   Place one ball on a well floured surface. Flatten dough and smooth edges with hands. Roll from center to edge forming a circle about 12" in diameter.

7.   Place pastry onto a 9" pie plate, repairing tears gently by pressing back together. Trim the edge of the pastry. Fold under the extra pastry (to reinforce the edge). Flute edge.

8.   Roll out second ball of dough. Place the mincemeat filling in the pie shell. Place pastry over filling. Trim the edge ½ inch beyond the edge of pie plate. Fold extra pastry under the edge of bottom crust. Flute edge.

9.   Cut slits in center (to allow steam to escape while baking). Bake in a pre-heated oven at 350°F for 20 to 25 minutes, or until golden brown.

Yield: 8 servings

	RCU	FU	Cal	%Fat	P	F	C	Na
Per Serving	0	½	322	11	7	4	72	220

Per Serving = 3 Fruit exchange; 1 Bread exchange; ½ Fat exchange

Pictured: Baked Turkey-Ham with Pineapple Raisin Sauce, Apple Baked Sweet Potatoes, Vegetable Medley, Fresh Garden Salad with De-Lites Holiday Dressing, Pineapple-Orange Pudding with Chilled Raspberries, p. 151

Menu Shopping List

Traditional Turkey Dinner with all the Trimmings Menu

Poultry

10-12	lb	young turkey

Produce

1	lg	red apple
1	med	banana
1		carrot
1	head	Iceberg lettuce
1	bag	fresh cranberries
1		cucumber
1	med	onion
2	lg	potatoes
2	sm	tomatoes
1	lg	yam

Dairy

1	pint	1% fat cottage cheese, reduced salt
1	pint	low-fat buttermilk
1	doz	eggs (6 eggs required)

Frozen

1	16oz	bag carrots
1	16oz	bag peas
2	12oz	cans apple juice concentrate
1	12oz	can apple-raspberry juice concentrate
2	12oz	cans Orchard Peach juice concentrate
1	12oz	can pineapple juice concentrate

Pictured: Fettuccine with Scallops Dijon, Fresh Steamed Asparagus and Sauteed Mushrooms, Buttery Oat Bran Muffins, and Apple Blackberry Cobbler, p. 166.

Flours / Powders / Starches
1	box	oat bran
1	sm	bag whole wheat flour
1	sm	container baking powder
1	box	baking soda
1	box	cornstarch
1	box	oat bran graham crackers

Miscellaneous Groceries
1	loaf	whole wheat bread
2	cans	low-fat evaporated milk
1	15oz	can small red beans
1	sm	bottle honey
1	sm	bottle vanilla
1	box	raisins
1	sm	can diced tomatoes
1	sm	jar dill pickles
2	16oz	cans fruit cocktail, in pear juice
1	sm	bottle almond extract
1	box	currants
1	sm	box dates
1	sm	bottle vegetable oil
1	15oz	can pumpkin
1	bottle	Butter Bud Sprinkles

Spices and Seasonings
1	sm	jar chicken bouillon granules, low sodium
1	bottle	onion powder
		salt
1	bottle	white pepper
1	bottle	Gifford's Basic Spice
1	bottle	Gifford's Dessert Spice

To order Gifford's Spices see form in the back of this book.

If not using Gifford's Spices review recipes for alternate spices required.

MENU

Baked Turkey-Ham with
Pineapple Raisin Sauce
Apple Baked Sweet Potatoes
Vegetable Medley
Fresh Garden Salad with
De-Lites Holiday Dressing
Pineapple-Orange Pudding with
Chilled Raspberries

Baked Turkey-Ham with Pineapple Raisin Sauce

This menu was created for the Easter Holiday, but would be great on any Sunday.

1	4lb	turkey-ham
2	C	pineapple juice, unsweetened, not concentrate
1	T	Gifford's Dessert Spice
½	C	raisins
1	T	crushed pineapple, unsweetened
2	T	cornstarch, mixed with ⅓ cup water
1	4oz	can pineapple slices, unsweetened, drained

Spice Substitute:

Instead of Gifford's Dessert Spice, substitute:

1½	tsp	ground cinnamon
1	tsp	ground cloves
¼	tsp	ground allspice

1. Place turkey-ham in a 9x9x2 inch baking dish. Pour pineapple juice over turkey-ham.

2.   Sprinkle Dessert Spice over turkey-ham. Bake in oven at 350°F for 50 minutes.

3.   Drain juice from turkey-ham into a saucepan. Keep turkey-ham warm. Bring juice in saucepan to a boil.

4.   Add raisins and crushed pineapple. Reduce heat.

5.   Slowly add cornstarch mixture stirring constantly until mixture thickens. Cook sauce on low heat 5 minutes.

6.   Place pineapple slices in a small skillet. Brown pineapple slices over medium heat.

7.   Remove turkey-ham from oven. On a cutting board slice turkey-ham into ¼ inch slices.

8.   Place slices onto serving plates. Place 2 pineapple slices over the turkey-ham. Spoon sauce over the top. Serve.

Yield: 16 servings; 2 slices turkey-ham each

	RCU	FU	Cal	%Fat	P	F	C	Na
Per Serving	0	1	191	28	22	6	12	885

Per Serving = ½ Fruit exchange; 2½ Meat exchange

Apple Baked Sweet Potatoes

2	lg	sweet potatoes, peeled and cut into 1½ inch pieces
2	qts	water
½	C	apple juice concentrate, unsweetened
2	tsp	Gifford's Dessert Spice
2	T	cornstarch, mixed with ½ cup cold water
2	sm	green apples, peeled, cored and cut in half, then sliced

Spice Substitute:

Instead of Gifford's Dessert Spice, substitute:

1	tsp	ground cinnamon
⅛	tsp	ground cloves
⅛	tsp	ground fennel seed

1. Place sweet potatoes in a large saucepan. Cover with the 2 quarts water. Bring to a boil.

2. Reduce heat. Simmer potatoes 15 minutes, or until tender. Drain (reserving 1 cup liquid).

3. Combine the 1 cup liquid, apple juice concentrate, and Dessert Spice in a small saucepan. Stir. Bring to a boil.

4. Add cornstarch mixture slowly, stirring constantly, until mixture thickens. Reduce heat at once.

5. Arrange potato pieces and apple slices evenly in a 9x9x2 inch baking dish. Pour sauce evenly over both.

6. Bake in oven at 400°F for 15 minutes. Serve using a slotted spoon. Ladle small amounts of sauce over potatoes and apples.
Yield: 6 servings

	RCU	FU	Cal	%Fat	P	F	C	Na
Per Serving	0	0	139	3	1	T	33	15

Per Serving = 1 Fruit exchange; 1 Bread exchange

Vegetable Medley

| 2 | 12oz | bags | frozen mixed vegetables |

1. Steam vegetables according to directions on package. Season with Gifford's Basic Spice if desired. Serve.

Yield: 4 to 8 servings

	RCU	FU	Cal	%Fat	P	F	C	Na
Per Serving	0	0	81	7	4	T	15	53

Per Serving = ½ Vegetable exchange; 1 Bread exchange

Fresh Garden Salad

1	med	head iceberg lettuce
1	sm	carrot, peeled, sliced thin
2	sm	tomatoes, cut in wedges
1	T	Gifford's Basic Spice

Spice Substitute:

Instead of Gifford's Basic Spice, substitute:

2	tsp	onion powder
1	tsp	garlic powder
1	tsp	ground thyme
½	tsp	black pepper
½	tsp	paprika

1. Remove core from lettuce head. Place lettuce head under cold water and rinse well. Drain thoroughly. Tear lettuce head into small pieces in a salad bowl.

2. Add carrots, tomatoes, and Basic Spice. Toss gently until mixed. Chill.

Yield: 4 servings

	RCU	FU	Cal	%Fat	P	F	C	Na
Per Serving	0	0	29	9	1	T	6	13

Per Serving = 1 Vegetable exchange

De-Lites Holiday Dressing

1	15oz	can red beans, without sugar
1	C	1% fat cottage cheese, reduced salt
3	T	Orchard Peach juice concentrate
½	sm	yellow onion
2	T	prepared mustard
1	T	Gifford's Basic Spice
½	tsp	Gifford's Mexican Spice

Spice Substitute:

Instead of Gifford's Basic and Mexican Spice, substitute:

2	tsp	beef bouillon granules, low sodium
2	tsp	onion powder
1	tsp	garlic powder
½	tsp	ground thyme
½	tsp	chili powder
½	tsp	ground cumin
⅛	tsp	ground cloves

1. Place red beans in a blender. Blend beans until completely smooth.

2. Add cottage cheese, Orchard Peach juice concentrate, onion, mustard, and spices. Blend ingredients until smooth (about 1 minute). Chill if desired. Serve.

   Yield: approx. 3 cups

	RCU	FU	Cal	%Fat	P	F	C	Na
Per ¼ cup	0	0	74	7	6	1	11	52

Per ¼ Cup = ½ Bread exchange

Pineapple-Orange Pudding with Chilled Raspberries

2	med	ripe bananas
1	lg	orange
1	C	raspberries, fresh or frozen, unsweetened
½	C	low-fat evaporated milk
½	C	water
½	C	Pineapple-Orange-Banana juice concentrate
1	tsp	banana extract
½	tsp	almond extract
1	T	dried orange peel
1	tsp	Gifford's Dessert Spice
4	T	cornstarch

Spice Substitute:

Instead of Gifford's Dessert Spice, substitute:

¼	tsp	ground cinnamon
¼	tsp	ground allspice
⅛	tsp	ground cloves
1	tsp	banana flavor extract

1. Place raspberries aside. Combine remaining ingredients together in blender. Puree until smooth.

2. Pour mixture into a medium saucepan. Cook over medium heat, stirring constantly for 10 minutes or until pudding mixture thickens

3. Pour pudding into serving dishes. As pudding starts to set, make a well in center by spooning pudding to the sides of dish. Place raspberries evenly in center. Chill if desired before serving.

    Yield: 6 servings

	RCU	FU	Cal	%Fat	P	F	C	Na
Per Serving	0	0	149	3	3	T	34	27

Per Serving = 2 Fruit exchange

Menu Shopping List

Baked Turkey-Ham with Pineapple Raisin Sauce Menu

Poultry
1	4lb	turkey-ham

Produce
2	lg	sweet potatoes
2	sm	green apples
1	head	Iceberg lettuce
1	sm	carrot
2	sm	tomatoes
1	bunch	green onions
2	med	bananas
1	lg	orange

Dairy
1	pint	1% fat cottage cheese, reduced salt

Frozen
1	12oz	can apple juice concentrate
1	12oz	can Orchard Peach juice concentrate
1	12oz	can Pineapple-Orange-Banana juice concentrate
1	16oz	bag red raspberries
2	12oz	bags frozen Mixed Vegetables (California Blend)

Flours / Powders / Starches
1	box	cornstarch

Miscellaneous Groceries
2	6oz	cans pineapple juice (not concentrate)
1	box	raisins
1	4oz	can pineapple slices
1	15oz	can crushed pineapple

1	15oz	can red beans, without sugar
1	sm	jar prepared mustard
1	can	low-fat evaporated milk
1	bottle	banana extract
1	bottle	almond extract

Spices and Seasonings

1	bottle	orange peel
1	bottle	Gifford's Dessert Spice
1	bottle	Gifford's Basic Spice
1	bottle	Gifford's Mexican Spice

To order Gifford's Spices see form in the back of this book.

Instead of Gifford's Spices:

1	bottle	ground cinnamon
1	bottle	ground cloves
1	bottle	ground allspice
1	bottle	ground fennel (grind whole fennel if necessary)
1	bottle	onion powder
1	bottle	garlic powder
1	bottle	thyme
1	bottle	black pepper
1	bottle	paprika
1	bottle	beef bouillon granules, low sodium
1	bottle	ground cumin
1	bottle	chili powder
1	bottle	banana flavor extract

Remember to check products you have on hand.

Seafood

MENU

Paella (Seafood and Rice)
Eggplant ala Acapulco
Chilled Clear Lime Gazpacho
Plantanos Fritos (Fried Bananas)

Paella (Seafood and Rice)

1	lb	fresh red snapper, cut into 1-inch pieces
1	sm	tomato, peeled and chopped
1	T	lemon juice
2	tsp	Gifford's Mexican Spice
2	C	mexican rice, cooked (Arroz Mexicano see recipe on page 10)

Spice Substitute:

Instead of Gifford's Mexican Spice, substitute:

2	tsp	chicken bouillon granules, low sodium
2	tsp	onion powder
1	tsp	chili powder
½	tsp	ground cumin
½	tsp	ground oregano
⅛	tsp	ground cloves
2	tsp	apple juice concentrate, unsweetened

1. In a skillet sprayed lightly with a non-stick spray, cook red snapper over medium heat stirring gently until done (about 5 minutes).

2. Add chopped tomato, lemon juice, and Mexican Spice. Blend gently

3. Add cooked rice. Stir gently to blend. Heat through about 2 minutes Serve.

Yield: 4 servings

	RCU	FU	Cal	%Fat	P	F	C	Na
Per Serving	0	1	659	9	80	7	65	261

Per Serving = 3½ Bread exchange; 6 Meat exchange

Eggplant ala Acapulco

This is my favorite vegetable recipe. If you haven't had much eggplant on your table, try this. I think you will really like it.

1	lg	eggplant
4	C	boiling water
½	C	fine wheat bread crumbs, dried
½	C	mozzarella cheese, shredded fine
1	T	Butter Bud Sprinkles
2	C	sliced mushrooms
2	C	tomato sauce, lite

1. Place whole unpeeled eggplant in about 4 inches boiling water. Reduce heat and simmer uncovered 10 minutes. Drain and allow eggplant to cool enough to handle.

2. Slice eggplant into quarters lengthwise, then peel each quarter. Cut into 1-inch pieces.

3. Mix bread crumbs and cheese together.

4. In a baking dish sprayed lightly with a non-stick spray, arrange half the eggplant pieces. Sprinkle half the Butter Buds over the top.

5. Add half the mushrooms, half the tomato sauce, then half of the cheese and bread crumb mixture. Repeat procedure for second layer.

6. Bake covered in a 350°F oven for 20 to 25 minutes. Serve.

    Yield: 4 servings

	RCU	FU	Cal	%Fat	P	F	C	Na
Per Serving	0	1	187	29	12	6	23	586

Per Serving = 2 Vegetable exchange; ½ Bread exchange; 1 Meat exchange

Chilled Clear Lime Gazpacho

2	med	tomatoes, peeled, cored, and peeled

Chef's Note: Blanch tomatoes for 30 seconds in boiling water. Run under cold water, then peel.

1	qt	chicken broth, low sodium
2	T	lime juice
2	T	pineapple juice concentrate
1	T	wine vinegar
1	tsp	Gifford's Mexican Spice
1		fresh lime, thinly sliced

Spice Substitute:

Instead of Gifford's Mexican Spice, substitute:

1	tsp	chili powder
1	tsp	onion powder
1	tsp	garlic powder
1/4	tsp	ground cumin
1/8	tsp	ground cinnamon

1.   Combine all ingredients except lime slices in a large mixing bowl. Stir to blend.

2.   Cover and chill. When serving, add lime slices to float.

Yield: 4 servings

	RCU	FU	Cal	%Fat	P	F	C	Na
Per Serving	0	0	68	24	3	2	11	89

Per Serving = 1/2 Meat exchange

Plantanos Fritos (Fried Bananas)

*Have you been looking for an alternative to sugar-packed snacks? Keep this recipe on
stand-by. It will satisfy "Mr. Sweet Tooth."*

2		green tipped bananas
2	T	apple juice concentrate, unsweetened
2	T	Grape Nuts, crumbed
1	T	Butter Bud Sprinkles
½	tsp	Gifford's Dessert Spice
1	tsp	ground cinnamon

Spice Substitute:

Instead of Gifford's Dessert Spice, substitute:

¼	tsp	ground clove
¼	tsp	dried orange peel
⅛	tsp	allspice

1. Peel bananas and cut in half lengthwise. Over medium heat, place
    bananas cut side down, in a skillet sprayed lightly with a non-stick
    spray.

2. Cook bananas 3 minutes or until golden brown. Turn over care-
    fully and cook 2 additional minutes, dropping the apple juice
    concentrate between banana halves.

3. Mix together the Grape Nuts, Butter Bud Sprinkles, Dessert Spice,
    and cinnamon. Sprinkle spiced mixture over bananas evenly.
    Serve.

    Yield: 4 servings; 1 banana half each

	RCU	FU	Cal	%Fat	P	F	C	Na
Per Serving	0	0	81	4	1	T	20	28

Per Serving = 1 Fruit exchange

Menu Shopping List

Paella (seafood and rice) Menu

Seafood
1	lb	fresh red snapper

Produce
3	med	tomatoes
1	sm	yellow onion
1	bud	garlic
1	lg	egg plant
8	med	mushrooms
1	med	lime
2		green tipped bananas

Dairy
1	sm	package shredded mozzarella cheese

Frozen
1	12oz	can pineapple juice concentrate
1	12oz	can apple juice concentrate
1	10oz	box frozen peas and carrots

Miscellaneous Groceries
1	sm	bottle lemon juice
1	sm	bag long grain brown rice
1	lg	can tomato sauce
1	bottle	Butter Bud Sprinkles
1	bottle	lime juice
1	sm	bottle white wine vinegar
1	sm	box Grape Nut cereal
1	sm	loaf whole wheat bread

Spices and Seasonings
1	sm	jar chicken bouillon granules, low sodium
1	bottle	ground cinnamon

1   bottle Gifford's Mexican Spice
1   bottle Gifford's Dessert Spice

To order Gifford's Spices see form in the back of this book.

1   bottle onion powder
1   bottle chili powder
1   bottle ground cumin
1   bottle oregano
1   bottle cloves
1   bottle allspice
1   bottle dried orange peel

Remember to check for products you already have on hand.

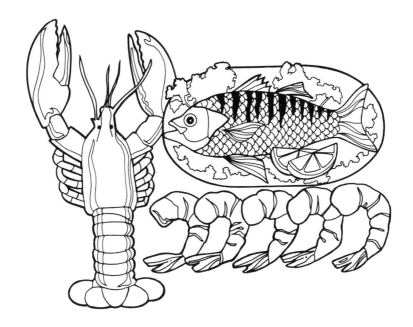

MENU

Fettuccine with Scallops Dijon
Fresh Steamed Asparagus and
Sauteed Mushrooms
Buttery Oat Bran Muffins
Apple Blackberry Cobbler

Fettuccine with Scallops Dijon

This recipe is much easier to prepare than it reads. Remember, having staple products on hand makes the whole process of cooking easier.

½	lb	Fettuccine noodles, cooked according to directions on package
½	med	white onion, diced
¼	C	clam juice
2	T	sauterne cooking wine, optional
1	C	water
2½	tsp	chicken bouillon granules, low sodium
2	tsp	garlic juice
1	tsp	Gifford's Italian Spice
1	tsp	Gifford's Basic Spice
1	tsp	onion powder
1	lb	scallops
3	T	cornstarch, mix together with ½ cup water
½	C	low-fat evaporated milk
1	T	dijon mustard
1	tsp	fresh parsley, finely chopped
1	tsp	diced pimentos

Spice Substitute:

Instead of Gifford's Italian and Basic Spice, substitute:

½	tsp	basil
½	tsp	thyme
⅛	tsp	paprika
⅛	tsp	white pepper
⅛	tsp	ground cloves

1. In a skillet sprayed lightly with a non-stick spray, saute diced onion over medium-high heat until onions appear clear.

2. Add clam juice and sauterne. Stir well.

3. Add water, chicken bouillon granules, garlic juice, Italian Spice, Basic Spice, and onion powder. Stir.

4. Add scallops and allow to simmer 5 minutes.

5. Add cornstarch mixture slowly, stirring constantly until mixture thickens. Reduce heat to low.

6. Add evaporated milk, dijon mustard, parsley, and pimentos. Stir gently until well blended.

7. Cook an additional 7 minutes. Serve over fettuccine noodles.

   Yield: 4 (4 oz.) servings

	RCU	FU	Cal	%Fat	P	F	C	Na
Per Serving	0	0	394	9	33	4	57	509

Buttery Oat Bran Muffins

See recipe on page 29.

Fresh Steamed Asparagus and Sauteed Mushrooms

½	lb	fresh asparagus
4		medium mushrooms, sliced
		water
dash		salt
		Gifford's Gourmet Spice

Spice Substitute:

Instead of Gifford's Gourmet Spice, substitute:

¼	tsp	dill weed
¼	tsp	garlic powder
pinch		ground cloves

1.   Remove woody bases from asparagus stalks by breaking stalks instead of cutting them. The stalk will snap where the tender part begins.

2.   Add a dash of salt to 1 inch of water in the saucepan. Bring to a boil.

3.   Add asparagus stalks to boiling water, standing the stalks upright in the pan. Cover and cook 12 minutes.

4.   In a saucepan sprayed lightly with a non-stick spray, saute mushroom slices over medium heat until tender. When serving, sprinkle Gourmet Spice over vegetables.

Yield: 4 Servings

	RCU	FU	Cal	%Fat	P	F	C	Na
Per Serving	0	0	17	8	2	T	3	61

Apple Blackberry Cobbler

This is a special, featured recipe, courtesy of Barbara Higa, R.D., author of Desserts to Lower Your Fat Thermostat. *This recipe is just one of her 200 delicious dessert ideas. Hey! My motto is "When you run across a good thing, share it with your friends."*

5	C	Rome Beauty, or other red cooking apples, peeled, cored, and thinly sliced (about 5 large apples)
1	C	fresh or frozen blackberries
1½	C	apple juice concentrate, unsweetened
3	T	cornstarch
1	tsp	cinnamon
1	C	granola (see next recipe)

Spice Substitute:

Gifford's Dessert Spice, substitute:

1   tsp   Gifford's Dessert Spice

1.   Combine apple concentrate, cornstarch, Dessert Spice, or cinnamon in a saucepan. Cook over medium heat until mixture comes to a boil. Add apple slices and blackberries.

2.   Place fruit mixture in a 7"x11" baking dish. Bake at 375°F for 25 minutes.

3.   Remove from the oven and sprinkle granola evenly over top. Bake for an additional 10 minutes.

Yield: 10 Servings

	RCU	FU	Cal	%Fat	P	F	C	Na
Per Serving	0	0	187	10	2	2	43	12

1 Serving = 2 Fruit exchange; ½ Bread exchange

Granola

2	C	rolled oats
2	C	rolled wheat
½	C	wheat germ
½	C	unroasted sunflower seeds, optional
¼	C	unsweetened apple juice concentrate, thawed
1	tsp	vanilla
¼	C	chopped dates
¼	C	raisins
¼	C	dried apples, cut into bite size pieces, optional
½	C	slivered almonds, optional

1. Mix together the oats, rolled wheat, and wheat germ. Add nuts if desired.

2. Combine apple juice concentrate and vanilla.

3. Blend all ingredients together. Put into a 9"x13" cake pan.

4. Bake at 275°F for 1 hour.

5. After taking granola out of the oven, add the dates, raisins, dried apples.

6. Use leftover granola as a cold cereal or mix with nonfat yogurt and fruit for a delicious breakfast.

Yield: 6 Cups or 8 (¾ Cup) Servings

	RCU	FU	Cal	%Fat	P	F	C	Na
Per Serving	0	0	263	9	8	3	55	9

1 Serving = 1½ Fruit exchange; 2 Bread exchange

Menu Shopping List

Fettuccine with Scallops Dijon Menu

Seafood
8	oz	fresh scallops (medium in size)

Produce
1	med	white onion
½	lb	fresh asparagus, --or--
1	12oz	bag frozen asparagus
4	med	mushrooms
5	lg	Rome Beauty , or Red Delicious apples
1	bunch	parsley

Dairy
1	pint	skim milk
1	doz	eggs (2 eggs required)

Frozen
1	12oz	can Mountain Cherry juice concentrate
1	12oz	can apple juice concentrate
1	16oz	bag frozen blackberries, unsweetened

Flours / Powders / Starches
1	sm	box oat bran
1	sm	box unprocessed bran
1	sm	container baking powder
1	sm	container baking soda
1	sm	container rolled oats
1	sm	container rolled wheat
1	sm	container wheat germ
1	box	fettuccine noodles (wheat or artichoke)
1	box	cornstarch

Miscellaneous Groceries

1	bottle	clam juice (check specialty foods section)
1	bottle	sauterne cooking wine (optional)
1	can	low-fat evaporated milk
1	sm	jar dijon mustard
1	sm	jar diced pimentos
1	sm	bottle vegetable oil
1	bag	unroasted sunflower seeds, optional
1	sm	bottle vanilla
1	sm	box chopped dates
1	sm	box raisins
1	bag	dried apples, optional
1	bag	slivered almonds
1	bottle	Butter Bud Sprinkles

Spices and Seasonings

1	sm	jar chicken bouillon granules, low sodium
1	sm	bottle onion powder
		salt
1	sm	bottle ground cinnamon
1	bottle	Gifford's Italian Spice
1	bottle	Gifford's Basic Spice
1	bottle	Gifford's Dessert Spice
1	bottle	Gifford's Gourmet Spice

To order Gifford's Spices see form in the back of this book.

Instead of Gifford's Spices:

1	bottle	allspice
1	bottle	banana flavor extract
1	bottle	basil
1	bottle	thyme
1	bottle	paprika
1	bottle	white pepper
1	bottle	ground cloves
1	bottle	dill weed
1	bottle	garlic powder

MENU

Louisiana Crab and Chicken Stew
Cornmeal Muffins and Onions
Fruit and Cabbage Salad
Peach and Pineapple Swirl

Louisiana Crab and Chicken Stew

When I featured this recipe on television, all of us at the station were taken aback at the enormous response. It's the most requested recipe to date. Enjoy!

1	lb	chicken breast tenders, cut into ½ inch cubes
1	16oz	bag frozen stew vegetables, thawed or (2 medium potatoes, cubed; 2 carrots, sliced ; 1 sm yellow onion, chopped and 2 sm stalks celery, chopped)
1	29½oz	can whole tomatoes, no salt, cut-up
1	C	tomato puree
3	T	clam juice
2	T	apple juice concentrate, unsweetened
1	T	worcestershire sauce
1	tsp	lime juice
2	tsp	chicken bouillon granules, low sodium
2	tsp	Gifford's Mexican Spice
¼	tsp	red cayenne pepper, to taste
½	lb	cooked imitation crab meat

Spice Substitute:

Instead of Gifford's Mexican Spice, substitute:

2	tsp	onion powder
1	tsp	garlic powder
½	tsp	chili powder
½	tsp	ground mace
¼	tsp	ground clove

1. In a large saucepan sprayed lightly with a non-stick spray saute chicken cubes over medium-high heat until cooked through, about 5 minutes.

2. Add remaining ingredients; stir well to blend. Reduce heat and simmer stew for 15 to 20 minutes. Serve.
    Yield: 6 servings

	RCU	FU	Cal	%Fat	P	F	C	Na
Per Serving	0	½	231	11	27	3	27	421

Per Serving = 2 Vegetable exchange; 2 Meat exchange

Cornmeal Muffins and Onions

It's my favorite muffin. I am a big cornbread fan so I may be a bit biased.

1¾	C	oat bran
1	C	yellow corn meal
1½	tsp	baking powder
½	tsp	baking soda
¼	tsp	salt
2	lg	egg whites, slightly beaten
1	C	skim milk
⅓	C	Orchard Peach juice concentrate
1	T	vegetable oil
½	sm	yellow onion, diced

1. In a mixing bowl combine oat bran, yellow corn meal, baking powder, baking soda, and salt; stir well to blend.

2. Make a well in center of flour mixture. Add remaining ingredients to the well. Stir to blend, but do not over mix.

3. Spray a teflon muffin pan lightly with a non-stick spray. Fill each cup ⅔ full with batter.

4. Bake in a preheated oven at 350°F for 25 to 30 minutes, or until golden brown. Remove from oven and allow to cool in pan 5 minutes. Remove muffins from pan. Serve.

    Yield: 12 muffins

	RCU	FU	Cal	%Fat	P	F	C	Na
Per Muffin	0	0	100	21	4	2	17	188

Per muffin = 1 Bread exchange

Fruit and Cabbage Salad

½	sm	head green cabbage, cut into 1-inch squares
1	med	carrot, shredded
1	med	banana, sliced
1	sm	apple, cored, quartered, then sliced
½	C	raisins
½	C	crushed pineapple, drained, reserve juice
1	C	1% fat cottage cheese, reduced salt
1	T	honey
2	T	Orchard Peach juice concentrate
½	tsp	vanilla
½	tsp	Gifford's Dessert Spice

Spice Substitute:

Instead of Gifford's Dessert Spice, substitute:

1	tsp	dried orange peel
½	tsp	ground cinnamon
¼	tsp	allspice
1	tsp	banana flavor extract

1. In a large salad bowl combine cabbage, shredded carrots, banana, apple, raisins, and crushed pineapple; stir gently to blend.

2. In a blender combine cottage cheese, reserved pineapple juice, honey, Orchard Peach concentrate, vanilla, and Dessert Spice. Blend until smooth, about 1 minute. Stir dressing into salad mixture gently. Chill if desired. Serve. *Yield*: 4 servings

	RCU	FU	Cal	%Fat	P	F	C	Na
Per Serving	0	0	198	5	9	1	42	248

Per Serving = 2 Fruit exchange; ½ Vegetable exchange

Peach and Pineapple Swirl

1	16oz	bag frozen peach slices
1	15oz	can pineapple chunks with juice, unsweetened
⅓	C	Orchard Peach juice concentrate
½	C	raisins
2	T	Butter Bud Sprinkles
1	tsp	Gifford's Dessert Spice
½	tsp	ground cinnamon
2	T	cornstarch, mixed with ½ cup cold water
2	T	Orchard Peach juice concentrate
1	C	De-Lites Cream Cheese (see recipe on page 14)

Spice Substitute:

Instead of Gifford's Dessert Spice, substitute:

1	tsp	dried orange peel
¼	tsp	ground cloves
¼	tsp	ground allspice
¼	tsp	ground anise seed
1	tsp	banana flavor extract
½	tsp	black walnut extract

1. In a skillet combine peach slices, pineapple chunks with juice, ⅓ cup Orchard Peach juice concentrate, raisins, Butter Buds, Dessert Spice, and cinnamon; stir to blend and bring to a boil.

2. Add cornstarch mixture slowly, stirring constantly until mixture thickens; reduce heat. Blend in the additional 2 tablespoons of Orchard Peach juice concentrate; remove from heat. Allow to cool a few minutes.

3. Add cream cheese and swirl into peach and pineapple mixture. Serve warm or chilled. *Yield:* 6 servings; about 4 ounces each

	RCU	FU	Cal	%Fat	P	F	C	Na
Per Serving	0	0	178	3	6	1	39	163

Per Serving = 2 Fruit exchange

Menu Shopping List

Louisiana Crab and Chicken Stew Menu

Poultry and Seafood
1	lb	chicken breast tenders
8	oz	cooked crab meat, --or-- imitation crab

Produce
2	sm	yellow onion
1	sm	head green cabbage
3	med	carrot
1	med	banana
1	sm	apple
2	med	potatoes
1	sm	celery

Dairy
1	doz	eggs (2 eggs required)
1	pint	skim milk
2	pints	1% fat cottage cheese, reduced salt

Frozen
1	12oz	can Orchard peach juice concentrate
1	12oz	can apple juice concentrate
1	16oz	bag peach slices, unsweetened
1	16oz	bag frozen stew vegetables

Flours / Powders / Starches
1	sm	box oat bran cereal
1	sm	box yellow corn meal
1	sm	container baking powder
1	sm	box baking soda
1	box	cornstarch

Miscellaneous Groceries

1	29oz	can	whole tomatoes
1	10oz	can	tomato puree
1		bottle	clam juice (check specialty food section)
1		bottle	worcestershire sauce
1	sm		bottle lime juice
1	sm		bottle vegetable oil
1	sm		box raisins
1	15oz		can crushed pineapple
1	sm		bottle honey
1	sm		bottle vanilla
1	sm		bottle banana flavor extract (optional)

Spices and Seasonings

1	sm	jar chicken bouillon granules, low sodium
1	bottle	red cayenne pepper
		salt
1	bottle	ground cinnamon
1	bottle	Gifford's Mexican Spice
1	bottle	Gifford's Dessert Spice

To order Gifford's Spices see form in the back of this book.

Instead of Gifford's Spices:

1	bottle	onion powder
1	bottle	garlic powder
1	bottle	chili powder
1	bottle	ground mace
1	bottle	ground clove
1	bottle	allspice
1	bottle	dried orange peel
1	bottle	ground anise seed

Remember to check staples and other items on hand before shopping.

Soup and Salads

MENU

Marinated Beef and Apple Salad with
Sweet Cucumber Dressing
Great Northern Bean Soup
Bill-O-Wee Apple Muffins
Apple-Butter Preserves

Marinated Beef and Apple Salad with
Sweet Cucumber Dressing

Sometimes on television things don't go quite as planned. I had this beautiful table set-
ting ready when I accidently bumped the soy sauce bottle. The lid was off. I tried to
recover, but here came this stream of sauce trickling down between the setting. Very, very
funny.

¼	C	lite soy sauce
⅓	C	apple juice concentrate, unsweetened
1	tsp	light olive oil
1	tsp	Gifford's Chinese Spice
1	tsp	paprika
½	tsp	Gifford's Dessert Spice
½	lb.	beef flank steak, cut into thin strips

1. In a bowl mix together all ingredients, except beef strips.

2. Marinate beef strips, in mixture, for 15 minutes.

3. In a skillet cook beef strips through over medium heat.

Spice Substitute:

Pictured: De-Licious Turkey Swiss Steak, Baked Hasselback Potatoes with De-Lites Sour
Cream and Chives, Finnish Cranberry Whip with Carrot and Celery Sticks, and Roasted
Pears with a Nut Cream Sauce, p. 210

Instead of Gifford's Chinese and Dessert Spice, substitute :

½	tsp	beef bouillon granules, low sodium
½	tsp	chicken bouillon granules, low sodium

½	tsp	ground ginger
½	tsp	ground mustard
⅛	tsp	ground cloves
½	tsp	ground cinnamon
¼	tsp	ground anise
¼	tsp	allspice

Apple Salad

1	med	red apple, quartered, then sliced
1	med	cucumber, peeled, membrane removed and sliced
1	stalk	celery , sliced
1	can	sliced water chestnuts, drained
2	C	shredded lettuce
		cherry tomatoes, optional

Dressing

1¼	C	1% fat cottage cheese, reduced salt
1	sm	cucumber, peeled, membrane removed, then chopped up
3	T	apple juice concentrate, unsweetened
3	T	pineapple juice concentrate
1	tsp	lime juice
½	tsp	Gifford's Dessert Spice
¼	tsp	paprika

Spice Substitute:

Pictured: Turkey Meatloaf Florentine with Mornay Sauce, Baked Seasoned New Potatoes, De-Lites Peas, Carrots, and Mushrooms, and Banana-Orange-Pineapple Sorbet with Raspberry Sauce, p. 234.

Instead of Gifford's Dessert Spice, substitute :

½	tsp	ground cinnamon
¼	tsp	ground allspice
¼	tsp	ground clove

4.   Combine dressing ingredients in a blender. Blend until smooth.

5.   In a large salad bowl combine the sliced apples, sliced cucumber, sliced celery, and sliced water chestnuts together. Toss gently. Add dressing. Stir gently to blend. Chill.

6.   Arrange ½ cup lettuce each onto 4 salad plates. Spoon apple mixture evenly over lettuce. Place 2 oz. each of the beef strips around apple mixture.

7.   Spoon remaining dressing over top of each salad. Garnish with cherry tomatoes and apple wedges if desired.

Yield: 4 servings

	RCU	FU	Cal	%Fat	P	F	C	Na
Per Serving	0	2	338	26	23	10	41	822

Per Serving = 1½ Fruit exchange; 2 Vegetable exchange; 2 Meat exchange; 1 Fat exchange

Great Northern Bean Soup

½	med	yellow onion, diced
3	stalks	celery , diced
2	15oz.	cans Great Northern beans, without sugar
1	sm	carrot, shredded
1½	T	Gifford's Basic Spice
1	C	tomato juice
3	T	Orchard Peach juice concentrate
2	tsp	worcestershire sauce
5	drops	tabasco sauce

Spice Substitute:

Instead of Gifford's Basic Spice, substitute :

1	tsp	bouillon granules, low sodium
1	tsp	chicken bouillon granules, low sodium
1	tsp	onion powder
1	tsp	garlic powder
1	tsp	ground thyme
¼	tsp	white pepper

1. In a skillet sprayed lightly with vegetable non-stick spray, saute onions and celery over a medium-high heat until tender.

2. Add beans, carrot, Basic Spice, tomato juice, Orchard Peach concentrate, worcestershire sauce and tabasco. Stir to blend. Reduce heat.

3. Simmer 10 minutes stirring occasionally. Serve.

Yield: 4 servings

	RCU	FU	Cal	%Fat	P	F	C	Na
Per Serving	0	0	322	4	20	1	61	89

Per Serving = 1 Vegetable exchange; 3½ Bread exchange

Bill-O-Wee Apple Muffins (by Chef Bill Gifford, my brother)

As the story continues (see Blueberry Turnover recipe) my brother, Chef Bill Gifford, really got into a creating mode. Here is a delicious muffin recipe as proof. The next problem was to give it a nice name. Bill-O-Wee is what he choose. I figured, "Well, why not?" Bill-O-Wee. I still chuckle.

1¼	C	whole wheat flour
½	C	dry non-fat powdered milk
¼	C	oat bran
1½	tsp	baking powder
½	tsp	baking soda
¼	tsp	salt
3	lg	egg whites, slightly beaten
2	tsp	vegetable oil
½	C	skim milk

¼	C	apple juice concentrate, unsweetened
½	tsp	black walnut extract
¼	C	raisins, chopped
1	sm	red apple, peeled, cored, diced
1	T	Gifford's Dessert Spice

Spice Substitute:

Instead of Gifford's Dessert Spice, substitute :

½	tsp	ground cinnamon
¼	tsp	allspice
¼	tsp	ground cloves

1. In a mixing bowl combine whole wheat flour, powdered milk, oat bran, baking powder, baking soda, and salt. Stir to blend.

2. In a separate bowl combine egg whites, oil, skim milk, apple juice concentrate, black walnut extract, and raisins. Stir well to break up the raisins.

3. Make a well in center of flour mixture. Add liquid ingredients to the well. Stir to blend.

4. Spray a 6 cup muffin pan lightly with a non-stick spray. Fill each cup almost to the top.

5. In a small bowl combine the diced apples and Dessert Spice. Stir to blend.

6. Make a well in center of dough in each cup.

7. Spoon spiced apples into well evenly.

8. Bake in a 400°F oven for 12-15 minutes, or until golden brown.

   Yield: 6 large muffins.

	RCU	FU	Cal	%Fat	P	F	C	Na
Per Muffin	0	½	211	11	10	3	39	318

Per Serving = ½ Milk exchange; 1 Fruit exchange; 1 Bread exchange

Apple-Butter Preserves

½	C	water
½	C	apple juice concentrate, unsweetened
2	T	Butter Bud Sprinkles
2	tsp	cornstarch, mixed with 2 T cold water
½	C	all natural apple sauce, unsweetened

1. In a saucepan bring the water and apple juice concentrate to a boil. Add Butter Bud Sprinkles. Stir.

2. Add cornstarch mixture slowly stirring constantly until thick. Remove from heat. Stir in apple sauce. Chill before serving.

   Yield: approx. 1½ cups or 12 (2 T) servings

	RCU	FU	Cal	%Fat	P	F	C	Na
Per Serving	0	0	26	2	T	T	6	3

Per 2 Tablespoons = ½ Fruit exchange

Menu Shopping List

Marinated Beef and Apple Salad Menu

Beef
| 1 | lb | beef flank steak, tenderized |

Produce
2		red delicious apples, 1 medium, 1 small
2	med	cucumber
1	sm	bunch celery
1	med	yellow onion
1	sm	carrot

Dairy
1	pint	1% fat cottage cheese, reduced salt
1	doz	eggs (3 eggs required)
1	pint	skim milk

Frozen
2	12oz	can apple juice concentrate
1	12oz	can Orchard Peach juice concentrate
1	12oz	can pineapple juice concentrate

Flours / Powders / Starches
1	sm	bag whole wheat flour
1	sm	bag dry non-fat milk powder
1	box	oat bran cereal
1	sm	container baking powder
1	box	baking soda
1	box	cornstarch

Miscellaneous Groceries
1	bottle	lite soy sauce
1	sm	bottle olive oil
1	can	sliced water chestnuts
1	sm	bottle lime juice

2	15oz	cans Great Northern beans, without sugar
1	12oz	can tomato juice
1	sm	bottle worcestershire sauce
1	sm	bottle tabasco sauce
1	sm	bottle vegetable oil
1	bottle	black walnut extract
1	sm	box raisins
1	bottle	Butter Bud Sprinkles
1	15oz	jar natural apple sauce

Spices and Seasonings

1	bottle	paprika
		salt
1	bottle	Gifford's Chinese Spice
1	bottle	Gifford's Dessert Spice
1	bottle	Gifford's Basic Spice

To order Gifford's Spices see form in the back of this book.

Instead of Gifford's Spices:

1	sm	jar beef bouillon granules, low sodium
1	sm	jar chicken bouillon granules, low sodium
1	bottle	ground ginger
1	bottle	ground mustard
1	bottle	ground clove
1	bottle	ground cinnamon
1	bottle	ground anise seed
1	bottle	allspice
1	bottle	onion powder
1	bottle	garlic powder
1	bottle	ground thyme
1	bottle	white pepper

Remember to check staples and other items on hand before shopping.

MENU

Fresh Garden Salad with De-Lites Ranch Dressing Hearty Mulligatawny Chilled Fresh Fruit (your choice) Peach & Pineapple Oat Honey Muffins

Fresh Garden Salad

1	med	head iceberg lettuce
4	leaves	red leaf lettuce
12		cherry tomatoes

1. Place lettuce under cold water and rinse well. Drain thoroughly.

2. Tear lettuce into pieces and place in a salad bowl. Toss gently.

3. Arrange salad evenly onto 4 salad plates. Place 3 cherry tomatoes around each salad. Chill if desired. Serve.

Yield: 4 salads

	RCU	FU	Cal	%Fat	P	F	C	Na
Per Serving	0	0	17	12	1	.2	3	9

Per Serving = ½ Vegetable exchange

De-Lites Ranch Dressing

1	C	1% fat cottage cheese, reduced salt
1	sm	dill pickle, kosher, crunchy, half salt
¼	stalk	celery, with leaves
2	T	Orchard Peach juice concentrate
2	tsp	dill pickle juice

1	tsp	chicken bouillon granules, low sodium
1	tsp	Gifford's Basic Spice
½	tsp	Gifford's Mexican Spice
¼	tsp	Gifford's Dessert Spice
1	tsp	prepared mustard

Spice Substitute:

Instead of Gifford's Basic, Mexican and Dessert Spice, substitute:

2	tsp	onion powder
½	tsp	garlic powder
½	tsp	ground thyme
¼	tsp	chili powder
pinch		cinnamon
pinch		ground cloves

1. Combine all ingredients in blender. Blend until smooth (about 1 minute). Chill before serving.

   Yield: 1½ cups dressing

	RCU	FU	Cal	%Fat	P	F	C	Na
Per ¼ cup	0	0	47	11	5	1	6	193

Hearty Mulligatawny

The wonderful blend of so many ingredients is surprising and makes this a choice dish.

4	C	water
6	oz	boneless chicken breast, cooked and then chopped
1	29oz	can whole tomatoes, no salt, cut-up (reserve liquid)
1	lg	red apple, peeled and cored
½	sm	onion, finely chopped
1	sm	carrot, finely chopped
½	med	bell pepper, finely chopped
1	sm	celery stalk, finely chopped
1	T	snipped parsley
2	tsp	lemon juice
2	tsp	apple juice concentrate, unsweetened
2	tsp	pineapple juice concentrate
2	tsp	chicken bouillon granules, low sodium
1	tsp	curry powder
¼	tsp	Gifford's Dessert Spice
¼	tsp	Gifford's Basic Spice
¼	tsp	Gifford's Italian Spice

Spice Substitute:

Instead of the Gifford Spices, substitute :

2	tsp	onion powder
½	tsp	ground clove
½	tsp	black pepper
1	tsp	chicken bouillon granules, additional

1. In a 3-quart saucepan or stock pot combine all ingredients. Bring to a boil. Reduce heat.

2. Simmer covered for 20 minutes stirring occasionally. Serve. *Yield: 4 hearty servings*

	RCU	FU	Cal	%Fat	P	F	C	Na
Per Serving	0	0	161	10	13	2	26	179

Per Serving = ½ Fruit exchange; 2 Vegetable exchange; 1 Meat exchange

Peach & Pineapple Oat Honey Muffin

1½	C	oat bran
1	C	rolled oats
½	tsp	baking powder
½	tsp	baking soda
¼	tsp	salt
2	lg	egg whites, slightly beaten
2	T	crushed pineapple
¼	C	Orchard Peach juice concentrate
2	T	honey
2	tsp	vegetable oil
1¾	C	skim milk
2	tsp	Butter Bud Sprinkles

1. In a large mixing bowl combine oat bran, rolled oats, baking powder, baking soda, and salt. Stir to blend.

2. Make a well in center of flour mixture. Add remaining ingredients to the well. Stir just to combine.

3. Spray a teflon muffin pan lightly with a non-stick spray. Fill each muffin cup ⅔ full with batter.

4. Bake in a 375° oven for 20 to 25 minutes, or until golden brown.

   Yield: 12 muffins

	RCU	FU	Cal	%Fat	P	F	C	Na
Per Muffin	0	0	105	18	5	2	18	196

Per Muffin = 1 Bread exchange

Menu Shopping List

Hearty Mulligatawny Menu

Poultry
1	6oz	boneless, skinless, chicken breasts

Produce
1	med	head iceberg lettuce
1	sm	head red leaf lettuce
12		cherry tomatoes
1	sm	bunch celery
1	lg	red delicious apple
1	sm	yellow onion
1	sm	carrot
1	sm	bell pepper
1	sm	bunch fresh parsley

Dairy
1	pint	1% fat cottage cheese, reduced salt
1	doz	eggs (2 eggs required)
1	pint	skim milk

Frozen
1	12oz	can Orchard Peach juice concentrate
1	12oz	can apple juice concentrate

Flours / Powders / Starches
1	sm	box Quaker oat bran cereal
1	sm	container Quaker rolled oats
1	sm	container baking powder
1	box	baking soda

Miscellaneous Groceries
1	sm	jar dill pickles
1	sm	jar prepared mustard
1	29oz	can whole tomatoes

1	sm	bottle lemon juice
1	sm	can crushed pineapple
1	sm	bottle honey
1	sm	bottle vegetable oil
1	bottle	Butter Bud Sprinkles

Spices and Seasonings

1	sm	jar chicken bouillon granules, low sodium
1	bottle	curry powder
		salt
1	bottle	Gifford's Basic Spice
1	bottle	Gifford's Mexican Spice
1	bottle	Gifford's Dessert Spice
1	bottle	Gifford's Italian Spice
1	bottle	Gifford's Chinese Spice

To order Gifford's Spices see form in the back of this book.

Instead of Gifford's Spices:

1	bottle	onion powder
1	bottle	garlic powder
1	bottle	ground thyme
1	bottle	chili powder
1	bottle	ground cinnamon
1	bottle	ground cloves
1	bottle	black pepper

Remember to check staples and other items on hand before shopping

MENU

Chicken and Peach Salad with Chilled Butter Lettuce
Cold Cucumber Soup
De-Lites Whole Wheat Bread & Berry Preserves

Chicken and Peach Salad served over Chilled Butter Lettuce

This was my first television recipe. Boy was I nervous! Imagine a crackling, talking ironing board with flashes of red. Ha!

1	lb	boneless, skinless chicken breasts, cut into ½ inch squares
1	tsp	chicken bouillon granules, low sodium
½	C	hot water
¼	C	Orchard Peach juice concentrate
1	16 oz	bag frozen sliced peaches, thawed
1	tsp	Gifford's Basic Spice
1	tsp	paprika
½	tsp	Gifford's Dessert Spice
2	T	diced pimentos
1	T	fresh chopped parsley
1	C	1% fat cottage cheese, blended until smooth
4	sm	heads butter lettuce (Boston Lettuce)
		cherry tomatoes, optional

Spice Substitute:

Instead of Gifford's Basic and Dessert Spice, substitute :

1	tsp	chicken bouillon granules, low sodium, additional for broth

When adding ingredients to blender substitute:

2	tsp	onion powder
1	tsp	ground thyme
½	tsp	ground cinnamon
¼	tsp	ground cloves

1. In a skillet sprayed lightly with a non-stick spray saute chicken over medium-heat until cooked through and browned, about 5 minutes. Add chicken granules to the hot water. Stir to make broth.

2. Add broth all at once to skillet. Stir.

3. Remove from heat and drain broth from skillet. Allow time to cool. Add to blender the broth and Orchard Peach juice concentrate, ½ of the peach slices, Basic Spice, paprika, and Dessert Spice. Blend until smooth.

4. In a bowl combine the remaining peach slices, chicken, ½ o f the pimentos, ½ of the parsley. Stir gently to blend.

5. In a separate bowl combine the cottage cheese and peach mixture from the blender. Stir to blend.

6. Rinse lettuce heads thoroughly. Drain. Trim core, so the lettuce will lay flat. Place heads onto 4 serving plates and gently spread out lettuce from the center using your fingers. Spoon chicken and peach mixture evenly over lettuce. Ladle dressing evenly over top of each salad. Garnish with remaining pimentos and chopped parsley. Add a few cherry tomatoes, if desired.

Yield: 4 servings

	RCU	FU	Cal	%Fat	P	F	C	Na
Per Serving	0	0	245	11	35	3	19	230

Per Serving = 1 Fruit exchange; 2½ Meat exchange

Cold Cucumber Soup

1	lg	cucumber, peeled, cut in half lengthwise, seeds removed
½	med	onion, diced
1	C	skim milk
2	T	red wine vinegar
2	T	apple juice concentrate, unsweetened
1	tsp	Gifford's Basic Spice
1	tsp	chicken bouillon granules, low sodium
1	tsp	dillweed

Spice Substitute:

Instead of Gifford's Basic Spice, substitute :

2	tsp	onion powder
½	tsp	ground oregano
pinch		nutmeg

1.   Slice half the cucumber into ¼ inch slices. Place remaining cucumber in blender.

2.   To blender add skim milk, red wine vinegar, apple juice concentrate, and spices. Blend until smooth.

3.   In a mixing bowl combine all ingredients. Stir. Chill before serving.

   Yield: 4 servings

	RCU	FU	Cal	%Fat	P	F	C	Na
Per Serving	0	0	68	6	3	.4	14	46

Per Serving = 1 Vegetable exchange

De-Lites Whole Wheat Bread

4	C	whole wheat flour
1¼	C	unprocessed bran
½	C	non-fat powdered milk

| 2 | tsp | Butter Bud Sprinkles |
| 1 | tsp | salt |

1. Combine in a large mixing bowl. Stir well to blend.

¼	C	apple juice concentrate, unsweetened
¼	C	Orchard Peach juice concentrate
1	C	water
2	T	honey
1	T	vegetable oil

2. Mix liquid ingredients together in a separate bowl.

| 1 | C | warm water |
| 1 | T | yeast |

In a separate bowl; dissolve yeast in warm water.

3. Preheat oven to 350°F. Spray 2 bread loaf pans with non-stick vegetable spray.

4. Combine yeast mixture with juices, oil and honey. Add dry ingredients. Blend well.

5. Place dough evenly into the 2 bread loaf pans. Let rise until almost double.

6. Bake loaves for 40 to 45 minutes.

7. Cool loaves on rack, in pan, for 5 minutes. Remove from pan. Continue to cool loaves on rack a few minutes. Slice loaves into ¼ inch slices.

Yield: approx. 10 slices per loaf

	RCU	FU	Cal	%Fat	P	F	C	Na
Per Slice	0	0	267	11	11	3	53	275

Per Slice = ½ Fruit exchange; 2½ Bread exchange

Berry Preserves

1	C	frozen berries, (your choice).
		Choose from raspberry, boysenberry, blueberry, blackberry.
½	C	apple-raspberry juice concentrate, unsweetened-OR-
½	C	Country Raspberry juice concentrate
½	C	water
2	tsp	Butter Bud Sprinkles
1	tsp	cherry flavor extract
1	T	cornstarch

1. Mix juice concentrate, water, cherry extract, Butter Bud Sprinkles, and cornstarch together in a small saucepan. Whisk briskly to blend.

2. Cook mixture over medium heat, stirring constantly until thick. Remove from heat. Stir in frozen berries.

Note: It's important to keep the berries frozen before adding them to the recipe. This allows the preserves to cool quickly and will keep them from setting into a gel. Store preserves in a container with a tight fitting lid. Gently stir preserves before serving.

Yield: approx. 1 pint or 16 (2T) servings

	RCU	FU	Cal	%Fat	P	F	C	Na
Per Serving	0	0	20	3	T	T	5	2

Per 2 Tablespoons = ⅓ Fruit exchange

Menu Shopping List

Chicken and Peach Salad Menu

Poultry
1	lb	boneless, skinless, chicken breasts

Produce
4	sm	heads butter lettuce (Boston lettuce)
1	sm	bunch fresh parsley
1	lrg	cucumber
1	med	onion

Dairy
1	pint	1% fat cottage cheese, reduced salt
1	pint	skim milk

Frozen
1	12oz	can Orchard Peach juice concentrate
1	12oz	can apple juice concentrate
1	12oz	Apple-Raspberry juice concentrate
1	16oz	bag peach slices, unsweetened
1	16oz	bag frozen berries (your choice)

Flours / Powders / Starches
1	5 lb	bag whole wheat flour
1	box	unprocessed bran
1	sm	box dry low-fat milk powder
1	pkg	dry active yeast
1	box	cornstarch

Miscellaneous Groceries
1	sm	jar chicken bouillon granules, low sodium
1	bottle	red wine vinegar
1	bottle	Butter Bud Sprinkles
1	sm	bottle honey

| 1 | sm | bottle vegetable oil |
| 1 | bottle | cherry extract |

Spices and Seasonings

1	sm	jar chicken bouillon granules, low sodium
1	bottle	paprika
1	bottle	dill weed
		salt
1	bottle	Gifford's Basic Spice
1	bottle	Gifford's Dessert Spice

To order Gifford's Spices see form in the back of this book.

Instead of Gifford's Spices:

1	bottle	onion powder
1	bottle	ground thyme
1	bottle	ground cinnamon
1	bottle	ground cloves
1	bottle	ground cloves
1	bottle	ground oregano

Remember to check staples and other item on hand before shopping.

MENU

Cherry Sweet and Sour Beef Strip Salad
Cream of Broccoli and Mushroom Soup
*Golden Brown Blueberry Muffins**
Mountain Cherry Butter Spread

Cherry Sweet and Sour Beef Strip Salad

½	lb	beef flank steak, tenderized, cut into thin strips
2	C	frozen cut broccoli
1	C	frozen pearl onions
1	sm	yellow pepper, cut julienne (if available)
1	C	quartered mushrooms
1	T	sliced pimento
4	C	shredded lettuce
		cherry tomatoes, for garnish
		grapes, for garnish

1. In a skillet that has been sprayed lightly with a non-stick spray, brown beef strips over medium-heat for about 5 minutes.

2. In a saucepan combine broccoli, pearl onions, yellow peppers, mushroom quarters, and pimento. Steam vegetables with a small amount of water until tender.

For Sauce

½	C	Mountain Cherry juice concentrate
¼	C	water
1	T	lite soy sauce

*Golden Bran Blueberry Muffins is a delicious recipe from *Gifford's De-Lites* Cookbook.

1	T	Butter Bud Sprinkles
½	tsp	Gifford's Dessert Spice
¼	tsp	ground mustard
1	T	cornstarch mixed with 3 T cold water

Spice Substitute:

Instead of Gifford's Dessert Spice, substitute :

| ½ | tsp | ground cinnamon |
| ¼ | tsp | ground cloves |

1. In a saucepan combine the Mountain Cherry juice concentrate, water, lite soy sauce, Butter Bud Sprinkles, Dessert Spice, and ground mustard. Stir to blend. Bring mixture to a boil.

2. Reduce heat and add cornstarch mixture slowly, stirring constantly until mixture thickens and becomes clear.

3. On 4 salad plates evenly arrange 1 cup shredded lettuce on each plate. Place 2 ounces of beef strips over lettuce on each plate. Spoon vegetables on both sides of lettuce and beef strips.

4. Garnish with cherry tomatoes and grapes. Ladle sauce over beef strips and vegetables. Serve.

    Yield: 4 servings

	RCU	FU	Cal	%Fat	P	F	C	Na
Per Serving	0	1	165	42	14	8	11	206

Per Serving = 1 Vegetable exchange; 1½ Meat exchange; ½ Fat exchange

Cream of Broccoli and Mushroom Soup

1	16oz	bag frozen cut broccoli
1	sm	onion, diced
6	med	mushrooms, sliced
3	C	water

1	T	Gifford's Basic Spice
2	tsp	chicken bouillon granules, low sodium
¼	tsp	Gifford's Dessert Spice
1½	T	cornstarch, mixed with ⅓ C cold water
1	C	low-fat evaporated milk
2	tsp	worcestershire sauce

Spice Substitute:

Instead of Gifford's Basic and Dessert Spice, substitute :

1	T	onion powder
½	tsp	garlic powder
½	tsp	basil
pinch		ground cinnamon

1. In a medium sized saucepan combine the broccoli, onion, mushrooms, water, Basic Spice, chicken granules, and Dessert Spice. Bring to a boil. Reduce heat. Simmer 15 minutes.

2. Add cornstarch mixture slowly stirring constantly until mixture thickens. Reduce heat to low. Add milk and worcestershire sauce. Stir and cook an additional 5 minutes. Serve.

   Yield: 4 servings

	RCU	FU	Cal	%Fat	P	F	C	Na
Per Serving	0	0	115	6	9	.7	20	131

Per Serving = ½ Milk exchange; 1½ Vegetable exchange

Golden Brown Blueberry Muffins

As the menu states, this recipe is from my first cookbook, Gifford's Gourmet De-Lites.
This recipe has been around a long time, but it's worth repeating.

1¼	C	whole wheat flour
¾	C	unprocessed bran
1½	tsp	baking powder
½	tsp	baking soda
¼	tsp	salt
2	lg	egg whites, slightly beaten
2	tsp	vegetable oil
¾	C	skim milk
¼	C	apple juice concentrate, unsweetened
½	C	frozen blueberries

1. In a small mixing bowl, beat egg whites with a fork, beat in oil, milk, and juice concentrate.

2. In a large mixing bowl combine the flour, bran, baking powder, soda, and salt. Make a well in center of the flour mixture. Add the egg mixture all at once. Stir gently just until blended. Fold in blueberries.

3. Spray a muffin pan with non-stick vegetable spray. Spoon mixture into muffin pan, filling each cup ⅔ full. Bake in 400°F oven 20 to 25 minutes.

    Yield: 12 muffins

	RCU	FU	Cal	%Fat	P	F	C	Na
Per Muffin	0	0	88	15	4	2	16	186

Per Muffin = 1 Bread exchange

Mountain Cherry Butter Spread

1	16oz	can pitted red tart cherries, packed in water, drained
⅔	C	Mountain Cherry juice concentrate
1	T	cornstarch, mixed with 3 T cold water
2	T	Butter Bud Sprinkles

| 1 | tsp | cherry flavor extract |
| 1/2 | tsp | almond flavor extract |

1. In a small saucepan bring the cherries and Mountain Cherry juice concentrate to a boil.

2. Add cornstarch mixture slowly, stirring constantly until cherry mixture thickens. Reduce heat at once.

3. Stir in Butter Bud Sprinkles and extracts. Cook on low for 5 minutes stirring frequently. Remove from heat. Let stand for a few minutes, then stir a little to blend. Serve warm or chill if desired.

Yield: approx. 1 pint or 16 (2T) servings

	RCU	FU	Cal	%Fat	P	F	C	Na
Per Serving	0	0	32	2	T	T	8	8

Per 2 Tablespoons = 1/2 Fruit exchange

Menu Shopping List

Cherry Sweet and Sour Beef Strip Salad Menu

Meat
1	8oz	beef flank steak

Produce
1	sm	yellow (bell) pepper
12-14	med	mushrooms
1	head	iceberg lettuce
		cherry tomatoes
		grapes

Dairy
1	pint	skim milk
1	doz	eggs (2 eggs required)

Frozen
2	16oz	bags frozen cut broccoli
1	12oz	bag pearl onions
1	12oz	can Mountain Cherry juice concentrate
1	12oz	can apple juice concentrate
1	16oz	bag frozen blueberries, unsweetened

Flours / Powders / Starches
1	box	cornstarch
1	bag	whole wheat flour
1	box	unprocessed bran
1	sm	container baking powder
1	sm	container baking soda

Miscellaneous Groceries
1	sm	jar diced pimentos
1	sm	bottle lite soy sauce (low sodium)
1	bottle	Butter Bud Sprinkles
1	can	low-fat evaporated milk

1	bottle	worcestershire sauce
1	sm	bottle vegetable oil
1	16oz	can red tart pie cherries, packed in water
1	bottle	cherry flavor extract
1	bottle	almond flavor extract

Spices and Seasonings

1	sm	jar chicken bouillon granules, low sodium
		salt
1	bottle	Gifford's Dessert Spice
1	bottle	Gifford's Basic Spice

To order Gifford's Spices see form in the back of this book.

Instead of Gifford's Spices:

1	bottle	ground cinnamon
1	bottle	ground cloves
1	bottle	onion powder
1	bottle	garlic powder
1	bottle	basil

Turkey

MENU

De-Licious Turkey Swiss Steak
Baked Hasselback Potatoes with
De-Lites Sour Cream and Chives
Finnish Cranberry Whip with
Carrot and Celery Sticks
Roasted Pears with a Nut Cream Sauce

De-Licious Turkey Swiss Steak

Mix together in a bowl:

½	C	whole wheat flour
1	T	Butter Bud Sprinkles
2	tsp	Gifford's Basic Spice
1	tsp	chicken bouillon granules, low sodium
4	4oz	fresh turkey breast slices
1	C	chicken broth, low sodium
½	sm	yellow onion, cut julienne
6	lg	mushrooms, sliced
2	tsp	Gifford's Basic Spice
1	T	cornstarch mixed with 3 T cold water
½	C	low-fat evaporated milk
1	T	pimentos
1	T	fresh chopped parsley

Spice Substitute:

Instead of Gifford's Basic Spice, substitute:

2	tsp	onion powder
1	tsp	garlic powder
½	tsp	basil
¼	tsp	white pepper

Blend until smooth.

1. Pour flour mixture onto a plate. Bread turkey slices thoroughly.

2. Preheat a skillet, on medium heat. Spray lightly with a non-stick spray. Place turkey slices in skillet; cook until brown on one side, adding small amounts of chicken broth around and between turkey slices while browning. Turn and repeat.

3. Add onions, mushrooms, remaining chicken broth and Basic Spice. Allow to simmer.

4. Add cornstarch mixture slowly until mixture thickens. Reduce heat to low. Add milk; stir. Cook 10 minutes. Add pimentos and parsley. Serve.

   Yield: 4 servings

	RCU	FU	Cal	%Fat	P	F	C	Na
Per Serving	0	½	245	10	33	3	22	133

Per Serving = ½ Vegetable exchange; 1 Bread exchange; 2½ Meat exchange

Baked Hasselback Potatoes

8	sm	new potatoes, scrubbed
		Gifford's Basic Spice to taste
		Butter Bud Sprinkles to taste

Spice Substitute:

Instead of Gifford's Basic Spice, substitute:

1	tsp	beef bouillon granules, low sodium
1	tsp	onion powder
1	tsp	garlic powder
1	tsp	paprika
½	tsp	black pepper

Sprinkle evenly over potatoes with the Butter Buds as called for in procedure.

1. Slice each potato in hasselback style, cutting to, but not through the bottom of each.

2. Place potatoes in a shallow baking dish that has been sprayed lightly with a non-stick spray. Sprinkle the Basic Spice and the Butter Buds over the top of each potato.

3. Bake in a preheated oven at 375°F for 40 minutes, or until done. Serve.

Note: Pull one side at a time off of hasselback, and dip in De-Lites sour cream (see next recipe) if desired. Delicious and easy to prepare, these potatoes make a great snack item.

   Yield: 4 servings; 2 potatoes each

	RCU	FU	Cal	%Fat	P	F	C	Na
Per Serving	0	0	38	4	2	T	8	13

Per Serving = ½ Bread exchange

De-Lites Sour Cream and Chives

2	C	1% fat cottage cheese, reduced salt
¼	tsp	vanilla
1	tsp	honey
1	tsp	unflavored gelatine, dissolved in 1 T hot water
1	T	onion powder
1	tsp	Butter Bud Sprinkles
2	tsp	dried chives

1. In a blender combine the cottage cheese, vanilla, honey, gelatine mixture, onion powder, and Butter Bud Sprinkles. Blend on mix speed until smooth.

2. Pour mixture into a bowl, or plastic container. Cover; chill for 1 hour before serving. Add dried chives to sour cream before serving, or sprinkle on top when serving.

   Yield: approx. 2¼ cups sour cream

	RCU	FU	Cal	%Fat	P	F	C	Na
Per ¼ Cup	0	0	45	10	7	T	3	205

Finnish Cranberry Whip

As a vegetable dip this one is right at the top. If you prefer this recipe a little sweeter, add 1 Tablespoon honey.

2	C	fresh cranberries
½	C	water
½	C	1% fat cottage cheese, reduced salt
½	C	apple-raspberry juice concentrate, unsweetened
1	tsp	imitation brandy extract
1	tsp	Gifford's Dessert Spice

Spice Substitute:

Instead of Gifford's Dessert Spice, substitute:

1	tsp	banana flavor extract
1	tsp	dried orange peel
½	tsp	ground cinnamon
¼	tsp	ground cloves
¼	tsp	allspice

1. In a saucepan bring the water to a boil. Add the cranberries. Cover; reduce heat and simmer 8 minutes.

2. Remove from heat and cool cranberries a few minutes.

3. Press cranberries through sieve to remove skins.

4. Combine ingredients in a blender. Blend on mix speed until smooth. Pour mixture into 4 serving cups; chill. Top off with De-Lites Cream Cheese (recipe on page 14). Serve with carrot and celery sticks.

Yield: 4 servings

	RCU	FU	Cal	%Fat	P	F	C	Na
Per Serving	0	0	108	5	4	1	22	125

Per Serving = 1 Fruit exchange

Roasted Pears with a Nut Cream Sauce

2	15oz	cans pear halves, in their own juice, drained, reserve juice
1	tsp	almond extract
1	tsp	black walnut extract
1	T	Butter Bud Sprinkles
1½	T	cornstarch, mixed with ¼ C cold water
2	T	low-fat evaporated milk
1	tsp	Gifford's Dessert Spice, to top

Spice Substitute:

Instead of Gifford's Dessert Spice, substitute:

½	tsp	ground cinnamon
¼	tsp	ground clove
1	T	crumbed Grape Nuts

Mix together in a small dish and use as directed.

1. Preheat a large skillet over medium high heat. Add pear halves to skillet. Cook until browned, turning occasionally.

2. Add juice from pears, almond extract, black walnut extract, and Butter Buds; stir gently to blend. Bring to a simmer.

3. Add cornstarch mixture slowly stirring until sauce thickens. Reduce heat to low; add milk. Stir to blend. Serve. Sprinkle Dessert Spice over the top.

Yield: 4 servings

	RCU	FU	Cal	%Fat	P	F	C	Na
Per Serving	0	0	94	1	1	T	23	26

Per Serving = 1 Fruit exchange

Menu Shopping List

De-Licious Turkey Swiss Steak Menu

Poultry
4	4oz	fresh, uncooked, turkey breast slices

Produce
1	sm	yellow onion
6	lg	mushrooms
1	sm	bunch parsley
8	sm	new potatoes
1	bag	fresh whole cranberries (2 cups)

Dairy
1	qt	1% fat cottage cheese, reduced salt

Frozen
1	12oz	can apple-raspberry juice concentrate

Flours / Powders / Starches
1	sm	bag whole wheat flour
1	box	cornstarch

Miscellaneous Groceries
1	can	low-fat evaporated milk
1	sm	jar diced pimentos
1	sm	bottle honey
1	sm	box unflavored gelatine
1	bottle	vanilla
1	bottle	Butter Bud Sprinkles
2	15oz	cans pear halves, in their own juice
1	bottle	imitation brandy extract
1	bottle	almond extract
1	sm	container dried chives (or fresh green onion slices)
1	bottle	black walnut extract

Spices and Seasonings

1	sm	jar chicken bouillon granules, low sodium
1	bottle	onion powder
1	bottle	Gifford's Basic Spice
1	bottle	Gifford's Dessert Spice

To order Gifford's Spices see form in the back of this book.

Instead of Gifford's Spices:

1	bottle	onion powder
1	bottle	garlic powder
1	bottle	basil powder
1	bottle	white pepper
1	bottle	black pepper
1	bottle	paprika
1	sm	jar beef bouillon granules, low sodium
1	bottle	banana flavor extract
1	bottle	orange peel
1	bottle	ground cinnamon
1	bottle	ground cloves
1	bottle	ground allspice

Remember to check products you have on hand.

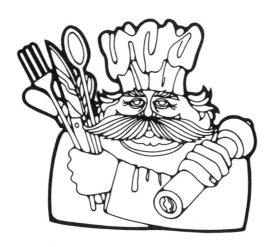

MENU

De-Licious Ravioli with Tangy Tomato Sauce
A Four Bean Salad
De-Lites Cheesecake with Razzleberry Compote

De-Licious Ravioli

This recipe takes longer than most of them, but after you go through the steps a few times, you'll have it down pat. Well worth the effort though, it's delicious.

Dough

2	C	whole wheat flour
1	C	oat bran
2	lg	eggs
6	lg	egg whites
1	tsp	salt
¼-½	C	water

1. In a mixing bowl blend the whole wheat flour and oat bran. Make a well in center. Add eggs, egg whites, and salt. Stir with a fork until just combined. Add water a tablespoon at a time, stirring until dough forms a ball.

2. Turn dough onto a well floured surface. Knead until smooth and elastic, about 5 minutes. Cover and let rest for 10 minutes.

3. Divide dough into 2 equal parts. (Cover dough to prevent drying.) Roll one part of the dough as thin as you can on a lightly floured surface into a 12-inch square. Trim to make square. Fold in half. (Cover with plastic wrap.) Repeat with second part of dough, but do not fold.

Filling

½	lb	ground turkey
½	sm	yellow onion, minced
1	clove	garlic, minced
1	10oz	package frozen chopped spinach, thawed, drained
½	C	Grape Nuts, finely crumbed
2	tsp	Gifford's Italian Spice
¼	tsp	Gifford's Dessert Spice

Spice Substitute:

Instead of Gifford's Italian and Dessert Spice, substitute:

1½	tsp	chicken bouillon granules, low sodium
1	tsp	onion powder
1	tsp	garlic powder
1	tsp	ground oregano
1	tsp	ground basil
½	tsp	ground thyme
¼	tsp	ground rosemary
¼	tsp	ground clove

1. In a skillet sprayed lightly with a non-stick spray saute ground turkey, onion, and garlic over medium-high heat until turkey is browned; remove from heat.

2. Stir in spinach, Grape Nuts, and spices. Mound 2 teaspoons meat filling 1½ inches apart in a checkerboard pattern on sheet of un-folded dough.

3. Dip a pastry brush in water. Brush in straight lines between mounds and edges of dough. Unfold the folded sheet of dough over the filled half. Starting at the center, press with fingers and side of your hand around filling and edges to seal.

4. Cut between mounds into squares using a sharp knife. Fill a large saucepan ¾ full with water. Add 1 teaspoon salt; bring to a boil. Add ravioli squares to boiling water. Stir gently to prevent sticking.

5. Cook uncovered until tender, about 12 minutes; reducing heat if necessary. Remove to strainer using a slotted spoon. Serve with tangy tomato sauce.

Yield: 6 servings; 3 ravioli each

Tangy Tomato Sauce

1	29oz	can whole tomatoes, reduced salt
1	15oz	can tomato sauce, lite
1	sm	onion, diced
2	cloves	garlic, minced
3	T	apple juice concentrate, unsweetened
1	tsp	chicken bouillon granules, low sodium
1	tsp	Gifford's Italian Spice
¼	tsp	Gifford's Dessert Spice

Spice Substitute:

Instead of Gifford's Italian and Dessert Spice, substitute:

1	tsp	onion powder
1	tsp	basil
⅛	tsp	ground clove

1. Place tomatoes, with liquid, in a medium saucepan, break up tomatoes. Add remaining ingredients; bring to a boil. Reduce heat. Simmer 15 minutes. Spoon over ravioli when serving.

Yield: approx. 1½ pints

	RCU	FU	Cal	%Fat	P	F	C	Na
Per Serving	0	1	400	12	28	5	67	881

Per Serving = 2½ Vegetable exchange; 3 Bread exchange; 1½ Meat exchange

A Four Bean Salad

2	C	shredded lettuce
1	15oz	can small red beans, unsweetened, drained
1	15oz	can garbanzo beans, unsweetened, drained
1	15oz	can great northern beans, unsweetened, no salt, drained
1	15oz	can cut green beans, unsweetened, no salt, drained
1½	T	wine vinegar
1	sm	onion, cut julienne
½	C	apple juice concentrate, unsweetened
¼	C	Pineapple juice concentrate
¼	tsp	Gifford's Dessert Spice
¼	tsp	Gifford's Gourmet Spice
¼	tsp	Gifford's Mexican Spice
¼	tsp	Gifford's Italian Spice
¼	tsp	Gifford's Chinese Spice
¼	tsp	Gifford's Basic Spice
		cherry tomatoes, or tomato slices to garnish if desired

Spice Substitute:

Instead of the Gifford Spices, substitute:

1	tsp	chicken bouillon granules, low sodium
1	tsp	beef bouillon granules, low sodium
1	tsp	onion powder
1	tsp	garlic powder
1	tsp	ground mustard
1	tsp	thyme
¼	tsp	ground cardamon
¼	tsp	dill weed
¼	tsp	chili powder
¼	tsp	ground cloves

1. Combine all beans, onion, juice concentrates, spices, and wine vinegar in a bowl; stir gently to blend. Chill.

2.   Serve buffet style, or arrange shredded lettuce on salad dishes.
       Spoon bean mixture evenly over lettuce. Garnish with tomatoes.
       Serve.

       Yield: 6 servings

	RCU	FU	Cal	%Fat	P	F	C	Na
Per Serving	0	0	333	6	17	2	64	233

Per Serving = ½ Fruit exchange; ½ Vegetable exchange; 3 Bread exchange

De-Lites Cheesecake

Preparing the crust will remind you of cutting butter into flour. The filling must be smooth and needs time to set. So chill it overnight as I've suggested.

For Crust

| 1 | box | oat bran graham crackers, crumbled |
| 4 | T | Orchard Peach juice concentrate |

1.   Separate crumbled graham crackers equally into 2 mixing bowls.
       Add 2 tablespoons of the Orchard Peach concentrate to each bowl.

2.   Using a large mixing spoon, cut into crumbs briskly until mixed
       and crumbs are flaky.

3.   Place crumbs from both mixing bowls into a round 8½ by 2½ inch
       baking pan that has been sprayed lightly with a non-stick spray.
       Spread crumbs evenly in pan until crumbs are ⅔ of the way up on
       the side of the pan. Press crumbs gently until crust is smooth.

Filling

1	15oz	carton low-fat Ricotta cheese
1	C	1% fat cottage cheese, reduced salt
⅓	C	Orchard Peach juice concentrate
2	tsp	honey
1	T	Butter Bud Sprinkles

1	tsp	lemon juice
1	tsp	lime juice
¼	tsp	vanilla
1	T	unflavored gelatin, dissolved completely in ¼ C boiling water

1. In a blender, combine all ingredients in the order given above. Blend on mix speed until filling is smooth, about 1 minute. A helpful hint: filling will become smoother easier if you keep the lid off the blender while mixing, and use a rubber spatula to gently skim the top of the mixture throughout the procedure.

2. Pour filling into crust. Place a sheet of plastic wrap gently over cake. Chill several hours before serving, overnight is best. Spoon razzleberry compote over top when serving.

Note: For a simple topping blend 1 cup Smuckers Simply Fruit preserves (your choice of berry), and 1 cup berries (to match you choice of preserve) in a small bowl. Spoon over cheesecake slices when serving.

Yield: 10 servings

	RCU	FU	Cal	%Fat	P	F	C	Na
Per Serving	0	1	196	27	10	6	27	262

Per Serving = ½ Fruit exchange; 1 Bread exchange; 1 Meat exchange; ½ Fat exchange

Razzleberry Compote

½	C	Mountain Cherry juice concentrate
½	C	water
1	T	Butter Bud Sprinkles
1	tsp	Gifford's Dessert Spice
1	T	cornstarch, mixed with ¼ C cold water
1	C	frozen boysenberries

Spice Substitute:

Instead of Gifford's Dessert Spice, substitute:

1	tsp	banana flavor extract
¼	tsp	ground cinnamon
⅛	tsp	allspice
⅛	tsp	ground cloves

1. In a saucepan; bring to a boil the Mountain Cherry juice concentrate, water, Butter Bud Sprinkles, and Dessert Spice.

2. Add cornstarch mixture slowly stirring constantly until mixture thickens. Reduce heat at once.

3. Add boysenberries; stir. Cook on low heat 5 additional minutes. Remove from heat and allow to cool before serving.

Yield: approx. 1 pint

	RCU	FU	Cal	%Fat	P	F	C	Na
Per ¼ Cup	0	0	44	3	T	T	11	5

Per ¼ Cup = ½ Fruit exchange

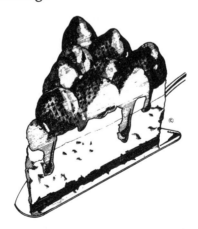

Menu Shopping List

Delicious Ravioli with Tangy Tomato Sauce Menu

Poultry
½	lb	ground turkey

Produce
3	sm	yellow onions
1	med	bud garlic
1	sm	head Iceberg lettuce
		cherry tomatoes (optional - for garnishing)

Dairy
1	pint	1% fat cottage cheese, reduced salt
1	15oz	carton low-fat Ricotta cheese
1	doz	eggs (8 eggs required)

Frozen
1	10oz	box frozen chopped spinach
1	12oz	can apple juice concentrate
1	12oz	can pineapple juice concentrate
1	12oz	can Orchard Peach juice concentrate
1	12oz	can Mountain Cherry juice concentrate
1	16oz	bag frozen boysenberries, unsweetened

Flours / Powders / Starches
1	sm	bag whole wheat flour
1	box	oat bran
1	box	cornstarch

Miscellaneous Groceries
1	sm	box Grape Nuts
1	box	oat bran graham crackers
1	bottle	Butter Bud Sprinkles

1	box	unflavored gelatin
1	bottle	vanilla
1	sm	bottle honey
1	29oz	can whole tomatoes
1	15oz	can tomato sauce
1	15oz	can small red beans, without sugar
1	15oz	can garbanzo beans, without sugar
1	15oz	can great northern beans, without sugar
1	15oz	can cut green beans, without sugar
1	bottle	lemon juice
1	bottle	lime juice

Spices and Seasonings

1	sm	jar chicken bouillon granules, low sodium
		salt
1	bottle	Gifford's Italian Spice
1	bottle	Gifford's Dessert Spice
1	bottle	Gifford's Gourmet Spice
1	bottle	Gifford's Mexican Spice
1	bottle	Gifford's Chinese Spice
1	bottle	Gifford's Basic Spice

Instead of Gifford's Spices:

1	bottle	onion powder
1	bottle	garlic powder
1	bottle	ground oregano
1	bottle	ground basil
1	bottle	ground thyme
1	bottle	ground rosemary
1	bottle	ground cloves
1	bottle	ground mustard
1	bottle	ground cardamon
1	bottle	chili powder
1	bottle	ground cinnamon
1	bottle	ground allspice
1	sm	jar beef bouillon granules, low sodium
1	bottle	dill weed
1	bottle	banana flavor extract

MENU

Breast of Turkey Tiffany
Lemoned Parsley Potatoes
Steamed Julienne Carrots
Oatmeal Muffin
Poached Pears in Sweet Red Sauce

Breast of Turkey Tiffany

4	2oz	slices uncooked turkey breast
½	C	whole wheat flour
½	C	water
⅛	C	frozen unsweetened Pineapple-Orange-Banana concentrate
½	tsp	onion powder
½	tsp	chicken bouillon granules, low sodium
1½	tsp	cornstarch mixed with 2 T water
3	T	skim evaporated milk

1. Coat turkey breast slices with flour.

2. Pre-heat a large skillet, sprayed lightly with a non-stick spray, over medium heat. Place turkey breast slices in skillet.

3. To brown, alternate the juice concentrate and water a teaspoon at a time . With each teaspoon, distribute evenly around edges of turkey slices. When golden brown on one side, turn turkey slices over. Repeat procedure.

4. Remove turkey slices from skillet. Place on a baking sheet. Keep warm in oven.

Sauce

1.   Pour remaining concentrate and water in skillet. Stir.

2.   Add spices. When mixture begins a rolling boil, add cornstarch mixture.

3.   Stir until sauce thickens. Add milk. Heat through. Serve over turkey breast slices.

        Yield: 4 servings

	RCU	FU	Cal	%Fat	P	F	C	Na
Per Serving	0	½	166	15	20	3	16	90

Lemon Spiced Parsley Potatoes

4	med	new potatoes
1	qt	water
1	T	lemon juice
1	T	dried lemon peel
1	T	Gifford's Basic Spice
1	T	fresh chopped parsley

Spice Substitute:

Instead of Gifford's Basic Spice, substitute:

1	tsp	onion powder
½	tsp	garlic powder
½	tsp	paprika
½	tsp	thyme
¼	tsp	black pepper

1.   In a medium saucepan combine potatoes, water, and lemon juice. Bring to a boil and cook potatoes about 15 minutes, until tender.

2. Remove potatoes from pan to a cutting board. Slice each potato into ¼ inch slices . Place on a serving plate. Sprinkle lemon peel, Basic Spice, and parsley evenly over potatoes.

    Yield: 4 servings

	RCU	FU	Cal	%Fat	P	F	C	Na
Per Serving	0	0	29	3	1	T	6	5

Steamed Carrots Marmalade

2	med	carrots, peeled, cut into sticks
1	C	Smuckers Simply Fruit Orange Marmalade
1	tsp	Gifford's Dessert Spice
1	tsp	dried orange peel

Spice Substitute:

Instead of Gifford's Dessert Spice, substitute:

2	tsp	Butter Bud Sprinkles
½	tsp	ground cinnamon
1	tsp	banana flavor extract

1. Place carrot sticks in a saucepan. Add enough water to cover carrot sticks; close pan tightly. Steam carrot sticks until tender, about 10 minutes.

2. Add marmalade, Dessert Spice, and orange peel. Stir gently to blend. Cook 5 additional minutes. Serve.

    Yield: 4 servings

	RCU	FU	Cal	%Fat	P	F	C	Na
Per Serving	0	0	228	1	1	T	61	24

Per Serving = 3 Fruit exchange; ½ Vegetable exchange

Oatmeal Muffins

1½	C	oat bran
1	C	rolled oats
1½	tsp	baking powder
½	tsp	baking soda
¼	tsp	salt
2	lg	egg whites, slightly beaten
¼	C	apple juice concentrate, unsweetened
2	tsp	honey
1½	tsp	vegetable oil
1¾	C	skim milk
½	tsp	black walnut extract
½	tsp	almond extract
½	tsp	Gifford's Dessert Spice

Spice Substitute:

Instead of Gifford's Dessert Spice, substitute:

½	tsp	banana flavor extract
½	tsp	ground cinnamon
¼	tsp	allspice

1. In a large mixing bowl combine the oat bran, rolled oats, baking powder, baking soda, and salt; blend well.

2. Make a well in center of flour mixture. Add remaining ingredients to the well. Stir gently until blended.

3. Spray a teflon muffin pan lightly with a non-stick spray. Spoon mixture into muffin pan, filling each cup ⅔ full. Bake in a 375°F oven 20 to 25 minutes, or until muffins are golden brown.

   Yield: 12 muffins

	RCU	FU	Cal	%Fat	P	F	C	Na
Per Muffin	0	0	97	18	5	2	16	196

Per Muffin = 1 Bread exchange

Poached Pears in a Sweet Red Sauce

From time to time when a health function or conference comes up, I'm asked to furnish a dessert recipe for the establishment to prepare and serve. This is my favorite. Its delicious and elegant in appearance.

2	15oz	cans pear halves, in their own juice
½	C	apple-raspberry juice concentrate, unsweetened
1	tsp	cherry flavor extract
½	tsp	almond flavor extract
1	tsp	Gifford's Dessert Spice
1½	T	cornstarch, mixed with ¼ cup cold water

Spice Substitute:

Instead of Gifford's Dessert Spice, substitute:

½	tsp	ground cinnamon
¼	tsp	ground nutmeg

1. Pour pear halves with juice into a saucepan. Cook over a medium heat 5 minutes.

2. Add apple-raspberry juice concentrate, cherry extract, almond extract, and Dessert Spice; stir gently to blend and bring to a simmer.

3. Add cornstarch mixture slowly, stirring constantly until sauce begins to thicken. Reduce heat at once. Cook an additional 5 minutes; serve.
   Garnish with fresh mint leaves or raspberries if desired.

   Yield: 4 servings; approx. 3 pears each

	RCU	FU	Cal	%Fat	P	F	C	Na
Per Serving	0	0	139	2	T	T	35	13

Per Serving = 2 Fruit exchange

Menu Shopping List

Breast of Turkey Tiffany Menu

Poultry
4	2oz	slices turkey breast

Produce
4	med	new potatoes
2	med	carrots

Dairy
1	doz	eggs (2 eggs required)
1	pint	skim milk

Frozen
1	12oz	can Orchard Peach juice concentrate
1	12oz	can apple juice concentrate
1	12oz	can apple-raspberry juice concentrate
1	12oz	can Pineapple-Orange-Banana juice concentrate

Flours / Powders / Starches
1	sm	bag whole wheat flour
1	box	cornstarch
1	box	oat bran cereal
1	sm	container rolled oats
1	sm	container baking powder
1	box	baking soda

Miscellaneous Groceries
1	sm	can low-fat evaporated milk
1	jar	Smuckers Simply Fruit Orange Marmalade
1	bottle	Butter Bud Sprinkles
1	bottle	banana flavor extract
1	sm	bottle honey
1	sm	bottle vegetable oil
1	bottle	black walnut extract

1	bottle	almond extract
2	15oz	cans pear halves, in their own juice
1	bottle	cherry flavor extract
1	sm	bottle lemon juice

Spices and Seasonings

1	sm	jar chicken bouillon granules, low sodium
1	bottle	dried lemon peel
1	bottle	onion powder
1	bottle	ground cloves
1	bottle	dried orange peel
		salt
1	bottle	Gifford's Basic Spice
1	bottle	Gifford's Dessert Spice

To order Gifford's Spices see form in the back of this book.

Instead of Gifford's Spices:

1	bottle	basil
1	bottle	white pepper
1	bottle	garlic powder
1	bottle	paprika
		black pepper
1	bottle	thyme
1	bottle	ground cinnamon
1	bottle	allspice
1	bottle	ground nutmeg

Remember to check for products you already have on hand.

MENU

Turkey Meatloaf Florentine with Mornay Sauce
Baked Seasoned New Potatoes
De-Lites Peas, Carrots and Mushrooms
Banana-Orange-Pineapple Sorbet with Raspberry Sauce

Turkey Meatloaf Florentine

Not just another meatloaf, its a gourmet meatloaf! Spinach haters will even like this.

1	lb	ground turkey
1	10oz	box chopped frozen spinach, thawed, drained
3	T	pineapple juice concentrate
3	T	unprocessed bran
2	lg	egg whites, slightly beaten
1	tsp	chicken bouillon granules, low sodium
1	tsp	Gifford's Basic Spice
1	tsp	Gifford's Gourmet Spice

Spice Substitute:

Instead of Gifford's Basic and Gourmet Spice, substitute:

1	tsp	chicken bouillon granules, low sodium, additional
1	tsp	onion powder
½	tsp	ground fennel
½	tsp	garlic powder
¼	tsp	ground cardamon
pinch		white pepper

1. In a mixing bowl, combine all ingredients.

2.   Place mixture in a 13x9x2 inch baking dish, that has been sprayed lightly with a non-stick spray. Pat to form a roll lengthwise from end-to-end.

3.   Add 1 cup water to bottom of pan. Bake in a 350°F oven for 45 minutes, or until done.

4.   Remove from oven. Drain juice from pan into a small saucepan for the Mornay sauce.

Yield: 4 servings

Mornay Sauce

juice		from meatloaf
⅔	C	water
2	T	finely diced onion
4	med	mushrooms, sliced
1	tsp	chicken bouillon granules, low sodium
1	T	cornstarch, mixed with small amount of cold water
⅔	C	skim evaporated milk

1.   Add water, onion, mushrooms, and chicken bouillon granules to left over juice in saucepan. Simmer until vegetables are tender.

2.   Add cornstarch mixture slowly stirring constantly until thick; reduce heat.

3.   Add evaporated milk; stir. Cook on low temperature for 5 additional minutes. Slice Turkey Meatloaf Florentine ¼ inch thick. Place on serving plate. Spoon sauce over top.

Yield: approx. 1 pint

	RCU	FU	Cal	%Fat	P	F	C	Na
Per Serving	0	½	246	9	36	3	21	209

Per Serving of Meatloaf with Sauce = 1 Vegetable exchange; 2½ Meat exchange

Baked Seasoned New Potatoes

8	sm	new potatoes
		Gifford's Basic Spice to taste

Spice Substitute:

Instead of Gifford's Basic Spice, substitute:

½	tsp	onion powder
¼	tsp	garlic powder
¼	tsp	thyme
¼	tsp	paprika
¼	tsp	black pepper

1. Moisten potatoes and prick with a fork. Sprinkle Basic Spice evenly over potatoes. Bake in oven at 375°F for 40 minutes. Serve.

    Yield: 4 servings

	RCU	FU	Cal	%Fat	P	F	C	Na
Per Serving	0	0	36	2	1	T	8	6

Per Serving = ½ Bread exchange

De-Lites Peas, Carrots, and Mushrooms

1	8oz	bag frozen peas
1	lg	carrot, peeled, sliced thin
4	lg	mushrooms, sliced
1½	C	orange juice

1. In a small saucepan bring orange juice to a simmer. Add carrot slices. Simmer carrots until tender.

2. Add mushrooms. Simmer 3 additional minutes. Add peas; heat through. Drain and serve. Season with Gifford's Basic Spice, if desired.

Yield: 4 servings

	RCU	FU	Cal	%Fat	P	F	C	Na
Per Serving	0	0	105	4	4	T	22	75

Per Serving = ½ Fruit exchange; ½ Vegetable exchange; ½ Bread exchange

Banana-Orange-Pineapple Sorbet with Raspberry Sauce

A filling dessert to end this cookbook. I hope you have great enjoyment with all of these recipes, for I truly have had much satisfaction in presenting them to you. Success is yours, and I wish you, and your loved ones, the best of health. Until next time, enjoy yourself. Your chef, Howard

⅓	C	low-fat evaporated milk
1	C	pineapple chunks
1	med	ripe banana, cut into 1-inch pieces
1	tsp	lemon juice
1	tsp	Gifford's Dessert Spice
1	tsp	dried orange peel
½	tsp	banana extract
1	tsp	vanilla

Spice Substitute:

Instead of Gifford's Dessert Spice, substitute:

½	tsp	ground cinnamon

1. Chill evaporated milk in freezer. Place pineapple and banana on a baking sheet. Flash freeze.

2. Place ½ the amount of pineapple and banana in blender; puree. Add the lemon juice, Dessert Spice, orange peel, banana extract, and remaining fruit; puree. Add ½ the amount of evaporated milk. Process until cream forms. Add remaining milk and vanilla. Process until blended.

3. Pour mixture into a freezer container. Freeze 4 hours. Remove from freezer and let stand for 10 minutes before serving. Spoon into dessert dishes. Pour raspberry sauce over top. Serve.

    Yield: 4 (3 oz) servings

Sauce

⅓	C	Country Raspberry juice concentrate
⅓	C	water
1	C	frozen raspberries, unsweetened
2	tsp	cornstarch, mixed with 2 T cold water
2	tsp	cherry flavor extract

4. Combine Country Raspberry juice concentrate and water in a sauce-pan; bring to a boil.

5. Add cornstarch mixture slowly, stirring constantly until mixture thickens; reduce heat.

6. Add frozen raspberries and cherry extract. Stir to blend. Remove from heat. Let stand at room temperature a few minutes before spooning over sorbet.

Note: Sauce can also be used as a berry preserve.

Yield: approx. 8-¼ cup servings

	RCU	FU	Cal	%Fat	P	F	C	Na
Per Serving	0	0	157	3	2	T	37	29

Per Serving = 2 Fruit exchange

Menu Shopping List

Turkey Meatloaf Florentine with Mornay Sauce Menu

Poultry
1	lb	ground turkey

Produce
1	sm	yellow onion
8	lg	mushrooms
8	sm	new potatoes
1	lg	carrot
1	ripe	banana

Dairy
1	doz	eggs (2 eggs required)

Frozen
1	10oz	box frozen chopped spinach
1	12oz	can pineapple juice concentrate
1	12oz	can Country Raspberry juice concentrate
1	16oz	bag red raspberries, unsweetened
1	10oz	bag peas
1	12oz	can orange juice concentrate

Flours / Powders / Starches
1	box	unprocessed bran
1	box	cornstarch

Miscellaneous Groceries
1	can	low-fat evaporated milk
1	15oz	can pineapple chunks
1	sm	bottle lemon juice
1	bottle	vanilla

| 1 | bottle | cherry flavor extract |
| 1 | bottle | banana flavor extract |

Spices and Seasonings

1	sm	jar chicken bouillon granules, low sodium
1	bottle	orange peel
1	bottle	Gifford's Basic Spice
1	bottle	Gifford's Gourmet Spice
1	bottle	Gifford's Dessert Spice

To order Gifford's Spices see form in the back of this book.

Instead of Gifford's Spices:

1	bottle	onion powder
1	bottle	ground fennel
1	bottle	garlic powder
1	bottle	ground cardamon
1	bottle	ground white pepper
1	bottle	ground black pepper
1	bottle	thyme
1	bottle	paprika
1	bottle	ground cinnamon

Remember to check products you have on hand.

Index

BEEF

Beef and Mushroom Sauce, 19
Beef and Vegetable Turnover, 17
Beef Strips in a Delicate
    Tomato Sauce, 33
"London Broil" with
    a Lite Beef Sauce, 24
Mexican Chili Verde, 8
Teriyaki Beef Tips with
    Whole Wheat Noodles, 2
Yankee Style "Pot Roast," 39

BREADS

De-Lites Whole Wheat Bread, 144, 196
Yeast Free Banana Raisin Bread
    with Golden Banana Topping, 131
Yeast Free Wheat Bread, 104

CHICKEN

De-Lites Chicken Picante, 94
De-Lites Gourmet Chicken, 101
Fried Chicken Steak with
    Country Gravy, 72
Hearty Mulligatawny, 190
Honey Almond Chicken, 64
No Oil Crispy Fried Chicken, 56
Old Fashioned Chicken
    and Dumplings, 48
Old Fashioned Chicken Pot Pie, 79
Roast Chicken with Chicken Gravy, 110
Roast Chicken with Plum Sauce, 86

DESERTS

Apple Blackberry Cobbler, 169
Banana-Orange-Pineapple Sorbet with
    Raspberry Sauce, 237
Berry Pudding Sauce, 82
Blueberries and Cream Turnover, 60

Bubbly Blackberry Cobbler, 90
Chilled Boysenberries and
    De-Lites Cream Cheese, 36
Chilled Clear Lime Gazpacho, 162
Crisp Apple Crunch Dessert, 76
De-Licious Bread Pudding, 98
De-Lites Cheesecake with
    Razzleberry Compote, 222
De-Lites Cream Cheese, 14
De-Lites Peach Cobbler, 42
Fresh Hot Mincemeat Pie, 146
Fresh Pumpkin Pie, 145
Hot Double-Crust Apricot Pie, 116
L'Orange and Sherry Sauce, 105
Mountain Cherries Jubilee, 30
Peach and Pineapple Swirl, 176
Pineapple-Orange Pudding with
    Chilled Raspberries, 155
Poached Pears in Sweet Red Sauce, 231
Quick Tapioca Pudding, 82
Roasted Pears with a Nut Cream Sauce, 215

DIPS

De-Lites Sour Cream and Chives, 213
Finnish Cranberry Whip, 214

DRESSINGS

De-Lites Basic Dressing, 142
De-Lites Green Goddess Dressing, 28
De-Lites Holiday Dressing, 154
De-Lites Ranch Dressing, 188
De-Lites Thousand Isle Dressing, 40
Lite Cherry-Lemon Dressing, A, 51
Sweet Cucumber Dressing, 181
Sweet Pineapple Dressing, 115

FRUITS

Honey Dew Melon Quarters and
    Blackberries, 81

Hot Fruit Medley with
  Crinkle Cut Carrots, 87
Peach Sauce and Halved Cantaloupe
  with De-Lites Cream Cheese, 69

GELATINS

Chef's Fruit Mold, 5
Fresh Strawberry Parfait, 21
Holiday Fruit Gelatin Salad, 130
Mandarin Orange Gelatin Dessert, 53
Pina Colada Parfait, 13

MUFFINS

Bill-O-Wee Apple Muffins, 183
Buttery Oat Bran Muffins, 29
Cornmeal Muffins and Onion Muffins, 174
De-Lites Hot Bran Muffins, 51, 124
Golden Brown Blueberry Muffins, 204
Oatmeal Nut Muffins, 230
Peach & Pineapple
  Oat Honey Muffins, 191
Sweet Spiced Oat Bran Muffins, 88

HAM

Baked Turkey-Ham with Pineapple
  Raisin Sauce, 151
De-Licious Eggs Benedict, 121
Spicy Turkey-Ham with
  Skillet Potatoes, 127

PASTA

De-Licious Ravioli, 218

RICE

Arroz Mexicano
  (Mexican Vegetable Rice), 11
Brown Rice and Mushroom Stuffing, 112
De-Lites Basic Spice Rice Pilaf, 88
Gourmet Spice Rice Pilaf, 102
Ham Fried Rice, 66
Spanish Corn Rice Pilaf, 95

SALADS

Cherry Sweet and
  Sour Beef Strip Salad, 201
Chicken and Peach Salad served
  over Chilled Butter Lettuce, 194
Chilled Endive Salad, 50
Chilled Green Goddess Salad, 27
Chilled Garden Salad, 141
Four Bean Salad, A, 221
Fresh Garden Salad, 154, 188
Fresh Tomato Slices
  on Red Leaf Lettuce, 20
Fruit and Cabbage Salad, 175
Fruit Cocktail Salad, 20, 143
Marinated Beef and Apple Salad, 180
Red Bean, Corn and Melon Salad, 12
Spicy Chinese Shrimp Salad, 68
Zucchini and Mushroom Salad, 114

SAUCES / PRESERVES / SPREADS

Apple-Butter Preserves, 185
Berry Preserves, 198
De-Lites Hollandaise Sauce, 122
Fresh Cranberry Sauce, 141
Golden Banana Topping, 133
Mountain Cherry Butter Spread, 204

SEAFOOD

Fettuccine with Scallops Dijon, 166
Louisiana Crab and Chicken Stew, 173
Paella (Seafood and Rice), 160

SNACKS

Granola, 170
Plantanos Fritos (Fried Bananas), 163
Smoked Cheeseball with Crackers, 128

SOUPS

Cold Cucumber Soup, 196
Cream of Broccoli and
  Mushroom Soup, 202
Great Northern Bean Soup, 182

SPECIAL DRINKS

Special Eggnog, A, 130
Special Orange Juice, A, 123

STUFFING

Onion Bread Stuffing (Dressing), 138

TORTILLAS

Baked Bean Tortilla Chips, 96
Tortillas De Harina
(Homemade Tortillas), 10

TURKEY

Breast of Turkey Tiffany, 227
De-Licious Turkey Swiss Steak, 210
Roasted Turkey and De-Licious
Turkey Gravy, 137
Turkey Meatloaf Florentine with
Mornay Sauce, 234

VEGETABLES

Apple Baked Sweet Potatoes, 152
Baked Hasselback Potatoes, 212
Baked Honey Butter Beans, 58
Baked Seasoned New Potatoes, 236
Crisp Chilled Chinese Vegetable Toss, 3
De-Lites Peas, Carrots and Mushrooms, 236
De-Lites Mashed Potatoes, 34
Eggplant ala Acapulco, 161
Fresh Steamed Asparagus and
Sauteed Mushrooms, 168
Fresh Vegetables and Gourmet Dip, 113
Fried Bean Sprouts and Mushrooms, 67
Golden Hashbrown Potatoes, 122
Lemoned Parsley Potatoes, 228
Old Fashioned Mashed Potatoes, 140
Pineapple-Oregano Zucchini, 97
Potatoes O'Brien, 74
Roasted Corn with Seasoned
Bread Crumbs, 59
Seasoned Whole Baby Potatoes, 26
Special Holiday Yam, A, 139

Steamed Asparagus with a
Spicy Mustard Sauce, 103
Steamed Broccoli with Creamy
Hollandaise Sauce, 35
Steamed Carrots Marmalade, 229
Steamed Carrots and Peas, 143
Steamed Crinkle Cut Carrots
in Pineapple Juice, 75
Steamed Cut Green Beans, 41, 52
Steamed Garden Peas, Pearl Onions,
and Pimentos, 116
Vegetable Medley, 153

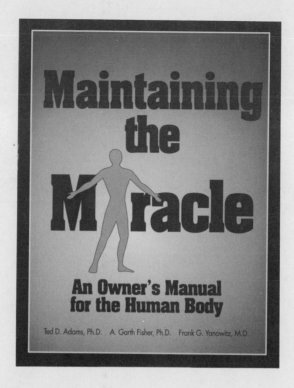

New, for the 1990's!

Anyone over 25 years old can not afford to be without this powerful asset. Professionals in health care praise its ability to make you a dynamic ingredient in your life long quest for wellness.

Maintaining The Miracle
An Owner's Manual for The Human Body

Your body is the most valuable possession you will ever own. Yet you may take better care of your car than you do your own body. In depth and up-to-date, this is the only book that tells you what to do and when to do it. You will thank yourself again and again for this invaluable help.

256 pages, 8½" x 11", Available September, 1991.

Easy Gourmet Menus
To Lower Your Fat Thermostat

The latest from Chef Howard Gifford, author of *Gifford's Gourmet De-Lites*. Low-fat gourmet cooking made easy. The 30 menus with over 150 irresistible recipes (including those presented by Chef Gifford on the popular Midday Show on KSL television, Salt Lake City, Utah) makes *Easy Gourmet Menus* a must for your cookbook library. Each easy to follow recipe gives the option of using his new conveniently packaged spice mixes, which you may purchase, or your own individual spices. Either way you'll be delighted with the taste of these wonderfully delicious meals.

Gifford's Spice Mixes

Chef Howard Gifford has just made your cooking easier. Now the unique flavors created by Chef Gifford can be had at the shake of a bottle. Eliminate the cupboard full of spices that are seldom used. But the time of mixing and measuring spices. No more guess-work to create a desired taste. These new spice mixes are conveniently packaged with six inviting flavors: Gourmet Spice, Mexican Spice, Basic Spice, Italian Spice, Chinese Spice, and Dessert Spice. Use these spice mixes with the delicious recipes in the new book *Easy Gourmet Menus to Lower Your Fat Thermostat* or flavor your own meals with the desired spice mix. You'll be delighted by the results.

Gifford's Gourmet De-Lites

Vitality House is pleased to offer you an exciting work from a professional chef, Howard Gifford, whose meals have astonished guests at weight loss health resorts. Says Howard, "I love to create that which is pleasing both to the eye and the palate. Preparing healthy food is my medium! My tools? The common everyday household conveniences found in most American homes today. 'Simplicity' is my watchword. Become the creative gourmet cook you have always wanted to be! Learn what the magic of using just the right spices, extracts and natural juices can do for your foods! I'll also give you some helpful hints for shopping and organizing."

How To Lower Your Fat Thermostat

Diets don't work and you know it! The less you eat, the more your body clings to its fat stores. This best-selling book contains the original program that teaches you to eat to lose weight. The *How To Lower Your Fat Thermostat* program is based on giving you plenty of nutrients and calories to convince the control centers in your brain to release excess fat stores. Your weight will come down naturally and comfortably, and stay at that lower level permanently.

Recipes To Lower Your Fat Thermostat

Companion cookbook to *How To Lower Your Fat Thermostat*. Once you understand the principles of the fat thermostat program, you will want to put them to work in your daily diet. Now you can with this full-color, beautifully illustrated cookbook. New ways to prepare more than 400 of your favorite recipes. Breakfast ideas. Soups and salads. Meats and vegetables. Wok food, potatoes, beans, and breads. Desserts and treats. All designed to please and satisfy while lowering your fat thermostat.

Acrylic Cookbook Holder

This acrylic cookbook holder is the perfect companion to your new cookbook. Designed to hold any cookbook open without breaking the binding, it allows you to read recipes without distortion while protecting pages from splashes and spills.

The Bitter Truth About Artificial Sweeteners

Research proves that those people using artificial sweeteners tend to gain more weight. Not only do artificial sweeteners enhance the desire for sweets, they also cause many unpleasant side effects in addition to raising the fat thermostat. Learn the real truth about artificial sweeteners and sugars. Learn how they affect your health and weight and what you can do about them.

Five Roadblocks to Weight Loss (Audiocassette)

If you have a serious weight problem that has failed to respond to the fat thermostat program, then you could be suffering from any of the five roadblocks to weight loss: food addictions, artificial sweeteners, food allergies, yeast overgrowth, and stress. Learn what these roadblocks are, what to do about them, and how the fat thermostat program relates to them . . . in an exclusive interview with Drs. Dennis Remington and Edward Parent.

Pocket Progress Guide

A pocket-sized summary of the fat thermostat program that includes food composition tables, daily records, and a progress summary for quick and easy reference and record-keeping anytime, anywhere.

Desserts to Lower Your Fat Thermostat

If you think you have to say goodbye to desserts, think again. At last there's a book that lets you have your cake and eat it too. *Desserts to Lower Your Fat Thermostat* is filled with what you thought you could never find: recipes for delicious desserts, snacks, and treats that are low in fat and free of sugar, salt, and artificial sweeteners.

The two hundred delectable ideas packed between the covers of this book meet the guidelines of both the American Heart Association and the American Diabetes Association. They will meet your own tough standards too -- especially if you've been longing for winning ideas that will delight your family without destroying their health.

Back To Health: A Comprehensive Medical and Nutritional Yeast-Control Program

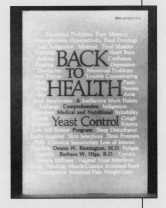

If you suffer from anxiety, depression, memory loss, heartburn or gas . . . if weight control is a constant battle . . . if you are tired, weak and sore all over . . . this book was written for you. While yeast occurs naturally in the body, when out of control it becomes the body's enemy, manifesting itself in dozens of symptoms. Getting yeast back under control can correct many conditions once considered chronic. More than 100 yeast-free recipes, plus special sections of weight control, hypoglycemia and PMS.

The New Neuropsychology of Weight Control
(8 Audiocassettes and Study Guide)

More than a million people have purchased the most powerfully effective weight control program ever developed -- *The Neuropsychology of Weight Control*. Thousands of them have reported dramatic and permanent reductions in their weight.

The New Neuropsychology of Weight Control program is a scientifically-based weight-loss system that teaches you how your body works and shows you exactly what to do to change from a fat-storing to a fat-burning metabolism. Still included are the proven principles from the original program based on the best-selling book *How To Lower Your Fat Thermostat*.

The New Neuropsychology of Weight Control program shows you how to set achievable weight loss goals and precisely what you need to do to reach them. You'll know how much weight you should lose and how long it will take. Included is a complete 12-week eating plan that provides daily menus, meal plans, tasty recipes, cooking instructions and eight shopping lists. You'll know exactly what to cook and how to cook it. And, you'll learn to create your own delicious meals that taste good while helping you to lose weight permanently.

The Neuropsychology of Weight Control
Personal Progress Journal

The journal will be your six month record of how well you're doing. By tracking your day-to-day progress you will ensure your long-term success.

The Will To Change
(Videocassette)

For some people, seeing is believing. While reviewing the key points of the program and the benefits of reaching your goal weight, this motivational video also features testimonials by people who have had dramatic success. In moments of doubt doubt or discouragement, this video provides the needed support and encouragement.

SyberVision's Neuropsychology of Self-Discipline
The Master Key to Success

There's one critical characteristic that makes the difference between success and failure: self-discipline. Without it, you can never hope to achieve your ambitions. With it, there's no goal you can't reach.

The Neuropsychology of Self-Discipline is a unique self-improvement program that allows you to instill a new and powerful self-mastery into your own mind and body. Armed with tools, insights, and skills of a highly disciplined achiever, you'll be able, perhaps for the first time in your life, to systematically pursue and successfully realize your most important goals.

QTY	CODE	DESCRIPTION	RETAIL	SUBTOTAL
	A	How To Lower Your Fat Thermostat	$ 9.95	
	B	Recipes To Lower Your Fat Thermostat	14.95	
	C	Acrylic Cookbook Holder	9.95	
	D	Neuropsychology of Weight Control (8 cassettes & guide)*	79.95	
	E	Back To Health (Yeast/Candida Guide)	9.95	
	F	Maintaining The Miracle (Available September 1991)	16.95	
	G	The Bitter Truth About Artificial Sweetners	9.95	
	H	Five Roadblocks To Weight Loss (Audiocassette)	7.95	
	I	Pocket Progress Guide	2.95	
	J	The Will To Change (Videocassette)	29.95	
	L	Neuropsychology of Self-Discipline (8 cassettes & guide)*	69.95	
	M	Personal Progress Journal (Sybervision weight program)	14.95	
	N	Desserts To Lower Your Fat Thermostat	12.95	
	O	Gifford's Gourmet De-Lites	12.95	
	P	Easy Gourmet Menus To Lower Your Fat Thermostat #	13.95	
	S	Gifford's Gourmet De-Lites Spice Mix Set #	20.95	
Shipping, 4th class book rate, $2.50 for the first item, $.50 each additional item.				+
For faster delivery, usually under five days, by UPS, add $1.50.				+
Canadian: $6.00 (U.S. dollars) for 1st item, $2.00 each additional item.				+
* Buy D or L and get 1 book free! Utah residents add 6.25% sales tax.				+
# Buy P & S together and receive $5.00 off your order!			TOTAL	$

Prices subject to change without notice.

Name_____

Address_____

City_____ State_____ Zip_____

Day Phone_____

☐ Check   ☐ Money Order   -   Make payable to **Vitality House Publishing**
☐ MasterCard   ☐ VISA   ☐ American Express

Card No._____Expires_____

Signature_____

How did you hear abour our products?   ☐ Friend   ☐ Book   ☐ Other _____

Mail to: 1675 No. Freedom Blvd. #11-C Provo, UT 84604 (801) 373-5100

Copyright© 1991 Vitality House International. Orders shipped upon receipt. Allow 2-3 weeks shipping.

EGM391

To Order: Call Toll Free 1-800-637-0708 or FAX 801-373-5370